Feeding the Cat
& other stories & poems

Rowan B. Fortune
(editor)

Published by Cinnamon Press
Meirion House
Glan yr afon
Tanygrisiau
Blaenau Ffestiniog
Gwynedd LL41 3SU
www.cinnamonpress.com

ISBN 978-1-907090-30-1
British Library Cataloguing in Publication Data. A CIP record for this book can be obtained from the British Library

Designed and typeset in Palatino & Garamond by Cinnamon Press
Cover design by Jan Fortune-Wood from original artwork supplied by agency: dreamstime.com

Introduction

Lindsay Stanberry-Flynn's winning short story *Feeding the Cat* recalls Alan Bennett's *Talking Heads*. The normality of its protagonist and his circumstances is belied by the psychological depth of the story itself. Pervading the story is a sense of isolation, loneliness, confused guilt and mortality—it is subtle and humane. All three of Stanberry-Flynn's stories are brilliantly observed, rooted in an understanding of the way peoples' internal lives surface in their behaviour. Rosemary Mairs' 'Thud' escalates without the softening effects of moralistic authorial intrusion; this and the harshness of her visceral details gives the piece an impact suggested by the title, but leaves the reader in a state of ambiguity, forcing us to engage with the events. Lezanne Clannachan's 'Monster under the bed' is a haunting, conversational narrative about the psychological constraints of fear; its uneventfulness, in contrast to 'Thud', emphasising the main character's desperate yearning for liberation, for action. *Feeding the Cat and Other Stories & Poems* is an anthology marked by such variety. What unites every piece in this book is only what unites every piece of good writing; they all involve the reader it a shared exploration of the human condition—whether through a dramatic encounter or a searching conversation.

This is just as true of the verse as it is of the prose. Aisling Tempany's light poem 'Academic Poet' conjures a humorous observation about a man that, 'Writes a three page poem for his dick/ And connects it to a national tradition./ He doesn't write smut, he writes culture.' Will Kemp, the winner of Cinnamon Press' tenth poetry competition, is concerned with how reality is experienced. In 'The end of the world' a lone worker in a deserted office room imagines the apocalypse, the poem hanging on a single 'as if', 'as if I was the sole survivor of a nuclear error,/ all my colleagues vaporised in a cloud of dust.' His poem sequence 'Thinking of Holland' remembers a lost romance and the landscape that contained it, ' I see broad rivers/ drift through/ endless plains/ rows of poplars/ tall and thin/ as smoke plumes/ far away.' These poems have a melancholy tone, 'I once heard that every life/ has a point before which there is/ always a looking forward,/ afterwards a looking back.'

Feeding the Cat and other stories and poems showcases emergent writing at its finest.

Rowan B. Fortune, April 2011

Contents

Feeding the Cat
& other stories & poems

Will Kemp

The end of the world

I am last at the office tonight, about to ping
a draft final report into the abyss of cyberspace.
The rows of desks have been left as they were,
the phones completely quiet, dead perhaps,
as if I was the sole survivor of a nuclear error,
all my colleagues vaporised in a cloud of dust.

Shortly I will leave for the car park, recording
my time of departure in the book on reception
like an entry at a funeral, then step out onto
the wet, still lit street, where there will be
no policeman on his beat, no smokers hunched
like conspirators outside The Wig And Mitre.

Without another car in sight, I will drive past
the outskirts of this northern town, stopping
at the garage for the milk you need for a cake,
helping myself to as much Premium Unleaded
as I like—and maybe some Mars Bars, crisps,
papers and barbeque charcoal since I'm at it.

Clutching my stash in one hand while waving
to the security cameras with the other, I will
at last head home—though starting to see now
the door will not open to KD Lang or Handel
playing throughout the house, nor will there be
any hint of the spicy noodles you had for lunch,

because this is the end of the world—that time
prophets with long beards and shaking fists
always said would come: no point in anything
anymore, everyone gone. No mug by the sink,
no note on the fridge; no chance either to ask
how your day was, or even say good-bye.

Harvesting at night

That low hum in the darkness becomes
a chatter throughout this prairie field—

the combine's arm extended like a claw,
long lights floating with corndust stars;

the driver lit up in his cabin too,
as if suspended in mid-air, or peering out

some submersible on the ocean floor,
watching for uncharted wrecks through

a shaken snow-globe of drifting silt,
where a deep sea fish might think him

a lost crustacean searching for a mate—
possibly the loneliest creature it ever saw.

Night flight to Frankfurt

We move through the night, a calculation in distance
over time, with variables of velocity, thrust and fuel;
the engines steady, no longer that whirlwind roar
at take-off—flare-white flashes from the undercarriage,
the runway's amber dots zipping by like tracer fire—

the same colour as the streetlit settlements of Holland
below, which glimmer like fissures in a lava flow
cooling to a mass of black rock, clouds wafting by
like dissipating steam. Something my father
wouldn't have seen as a young navigator faced with

his first mission, yet this is the route he trained for:
east-south-east to Arnhem, the moonlit wire
of the Rhine and the Ruhr, the drop-zone over Köln,
heavy flak coming up around Essen. No practice runs
anymore—no leg-room either, or an automatic pilot

to find a way through the dark – only checks of altitude,
windspeed, bearings on charts. No wish to put up
a good show, or teach Gerry a lesson, just to get home
without Messerschmidts at two o'clock, ice jamming
the tail-flap; and all the time wanting nothing more than

to sit back as I do now, above an Autobahn joining
the pearls of a Ringstrasse—where people will soon
be walking their dogs, children going to school—
the pale lights of some city rising in the distance
like dawn, instead of a smouldering ruin.

Thinking of Holland

I The light on the water at Rhenen

It was a Saturday in July —
the sky pale but open wide;
typically Dutch, you said,
an unhurried cloud passing by.

We sat on rough grass,
you in my sweater, if I remember,
bicycle wheels still spinning,
ticking, by the water's edge.

The river slapped and plopped
again and again. Further out,
it seemed to glitter silver
the way leaves do after rain.

We watched a *kahn* inch forward,
lugging coal to Koblenz or Köln,
a line of shirts in surrender
from bridge to stern.

I put my head on your lap,
and you fed me apricot Limburg Flan —
but only after I'd said
sinaasappelsap.

You explained polders, dykes,
the need to maintain the water level.
I kept quiet about the way
your father looked at me that morning.

I once heard that every life
has a point before which there is
always a looking forward,
afterwards a looking back.

These are the things I think of,
whenever I think of that.

II The things you gave me

I still have the things you gave me,
hidden in a secret place.
Letters tell how we used to be,
photos let me touch your face.

Hidden in a secret place,
a fake tulip brings back the past.
Photos let me touch your face,
the poems you sent let love last.

A fake tulip brings back the past.
Letters tell how we used to be.
The poems you sent let love last.
I still have the things you gave me.

III Thinking of Holland

after the poem Herinnering aan Holland by Hendrik Marsman (1936)

I see broad rivers
drift through
endless plains
rows of poplars
tall and thin
as smoke plumes
far away

and throughout
that sunken space
woods farms fields
churches elms
both scattered
and as one

the sun is low
and sinks through
a mist spun from
different greys
towards the water
where the cries
from long ago
are still heard
and feared

The Young Man with the Nose Ring and Gloria
Lindsay Stanberry-Flynn

Frances strides into the bar. She hardly ever strides. Sidle is a better word to describe her approach to life. She has only ever taken one bold decision and look where that got her. But today, because she is late and because her heart is flipping somersaults, Frances strides.

It is one of those new bars: wooden floors, high ceilings, sofas, lots of glass, the sort of place Frances hates. She chose it because she thought Patrick might like it, the vibrant atmosphere, its sense of something happening.

That's what he always used to say when he rang, 'What's happening?'

She came to dread the question, however much she longed for the call. 'Not a lot,' she'd say. 'What about you?'

'This and that. Places to go. People to see.' It was the closest she ever got.

Frances scans the bar. There's no sign of Patrick, but a group in the far corner stands up and she makes a beeline for their table. Beeline, stride—she really is acting out of character today. As she perches on a chair, four glasses of lager crash down on the table next to her. Pale yellow liquid slops across the pine surface.

One of the young men turns to smile at her. 'Really sorry.' He is wearing a long black overcoat and big boots. His blond hair stands up from his head like miniature sheaves of wheat. Aggressive-looking studs line his ears and eyebrows and a ring hangs from his right nostril. His eyes are circled with black make up.

He is the sort of person Frances normally shies away from, but his smile eases the pain in her stomach, and she settles her handbag on the bench between them.

Patrick is late. But she's used to that.

'See you later,' he would say and at first she believed him. Waited up for him, fretted as hours and sometimes days passed.

'I worry about you.' She knew that irritated him, but she couldn't stop herself.

'Don't. I'll be fine. See you later.'

And always, usually just as she'd abandoned her vigil behind the white nets, he turned up. Fine. As he had promised.

Frances is aware that her lap feels damp. She looks down. Lager is dripping from the puddle on the table on to her smart blue suit. It seemed a good idea this morning—up at six, unable to sleep, freshly showered, crisp white shirt, new suit. Frances told herself she had caught the right note, smiled when Mrs White next door looked up from her daily sweeping of the garden path. 'Mmm. Very smart. Off somewhere special are we?' Now she feels ridiculous.

Next to her the young man with the ear and eyebrow studs is holding out a napkin.

'Sorry about that,' he says again.

She takes the napkin, flinching from the nicotine-stained fingers.

'It's always packed in here. Do you want to get yourself a drink? I'll keep your place.'

Frances looks across to the crowded bar. She doesn't usually drink, but a sweet sherry might calm her nerves. She sees a space where she could stand without having to push her way through, but as she decides, a young girl with bright orange hair slips into it.

She turns back to the young man, shaking her head. Her eyes are fixed on the fleshy skin of his right nostril. It's sore and inflamed-looking around the ring.

'I'm waiting for my son.'

'Late is he? My mum says I'll be late for my own funeral.'

'I haven't seen him for nine years.' The words are out of Frances's mouth before she can stop herself. She can't believe she has said them, especially to a stranger whose appearance is so scary. But a burst of laughter at the other end of the table has recalled the young man to his friends and he doesn't seem to have heard.

Frances is relieved. She's always afraid she'll say the wrong thing. But then she's afraid of so many things. Afraid she might open her purse in the supermarket and find she has no money, afraid of the telephone bell late at night... 'You—you're frightened of your own shadow,' Harry used to say.

But she was brave once. Just that once she made such a brave decision and it changed her life. Harry left her for a start.

'We're off now.' The young men next to her stand up. The one with the blond hair smiles at her again. 'Hope he turns up soon...

17

your son, I mean.'

Frances finds herself smiling back. She wants to ask him about the studs. Do they hurt? What happens when he has a cold? But he is already moving away. She fingers her own earlobes. Perhaps she should have hers pierced.

'Hello Mum.'

My baby was born in the early hours of the morning at The Royal Northern Hospital, Holloway, on 17th January 1961. He was three months early and he died six hours later. I didn't see him, didn't hold him, didn't hear him cry. It was almost as if he had never existed. The birth was an emergency, a caesarean section. When they opened me up, they found a tumour as big as an orange. There would be no more babies, they said.

Harry visited me that evening. He tried to be sympathetic, but it was never his strong point.

'Think of all the money and trouble we'll save.' He rubbed his hand up and down my arm in what I'm sure he thought was a gesture of tenderness, but the pain from my stomach wound had seeped into every part of my body and the rough skin of his palm was one ache too many. I hoped he would go soon. I could tell he felt the same. His eyes flitted from side to side as he searched the ward for something more interesting than me to look at.

'Trust you to end up next to a wog!' He jerked his head across to the next bed.

I had been too sleepy from the anaesthetic to notice, but now I glanced across to find the woman in the adjacent bed smiling at me, her white teeth gleaming against her brown skin.

When Harry left, she got out of bed and came across to me.

'I'm so sorry about your son.'

My son, she'd called him. For the first time he seemed real. Tears filled my eyes, and she reached out to touch my hand. I looked down at my pale freckly skin, unhealthy and pallid, next to her warm teak glow. I had never been so close to a coloured person. I'd seen them, of course. There was the bus conductor with his pink-tipped fingers and pink palms, the porter at Upper Holloway station whose broad flat feet, flapping in his unlaced shoes, made us laugh. Jungle feet, we called them. But I had never actually met one, not properly. The woman saw my glance and took her hand away.

'Please,' I said, 'can I see your baby?'

She reached into the cot by her bed. A mass of black frizzy hair appeared above the cream woollen blanket. She stood next to my bed, rocking the baby, crooning gently.

'I wanted a boy,' she said. 'Life is too hard for girls.'

The soft rise and fall of her accent, the laughter in her voice soothed me and I stretched out my arms. 'Can I hold him?'

She helped me get comfortable with a pillow across my stomach and lowered her baby son into my embrace. He was darker than his mother and the skin on his cheeks was like mahogany, lustrous with years of loving polish. His pupils were very black against the milky whiteness of the iris.

'He's beautiful. What's his name?'

'Patrice.'

'That's nice. After your husband?'

'No. After Lumumba.'

I felt stupid. Who was Lumumba? Her dad? But it sounded like a place. Harry said coloured women were promiscuous. Maybe she had another chap.

She saw the hesitation in my face. 'Patrice Lumumba, President of the Congo.'

'The Congo? I didn't know where she meant. I'd never taken much notice of the world.

'He's in prison.' Her voice grew hard. 'My husband's gone back to fight for him. Who knows when he'll see little Patrice? But he said if it's a boy that's what I must call him.' She lifted the baby from my arms, leaving only the imprint of his small body on the pillow.

Over the next few days I grew stronger. So too, to my surprise, did my friendship with the coloured woman. Her name was Gloria and she was from Jamaica. She had come to England when she was fourteen with her mother. It was 1953, 'The year of your glorious Queen's coronation'. Her father had arrived the year before and sent for them. When she was eighteen, her parents returned home, unable to cope with the weather and the cruelty of life in England. I didn't know what to say to that, so I let her go on talking, captivated by her sing-song voice and black dancing eyes.

'They said I had to go with them. Momma cried, Pappi beat me, big as I was, but I'd met Francois by then and I was in love.'

Francois was from the Belgian Congo and had come to

England to study medicine, Gloria said. He was going to be a doctor when Lumumba's Congo became independent. So many names, so many strange words, my head whirled. But her voice softened my pain and I silently urged her on.

She had waved her parents off at Southampton and she hadn't seen them since. 'Momma used to write, but when Francois and I got married, that was it. Pappi wouldn't let her any more.'

'Why didn't they like Francois?' I asked.

She shrugged. 'Who knows? Because he's from Africa. Because he's different. Because they were frightened he'd take me back to the Congo with him and they'd lose me.'

'Do they know about the baby?'

'No. Nor will they. As soon as Patrice is old enough, we'll join Francois.'

One morning, I woke to the sound of sobbing. It was Gloria. I went to her bed and held her hand, as she had held mine. Her blackness didn't seem strange any more.

'It's the three day blues,' I told her. 'It will pass.'

She shook her head. 'It's Lumumba. They killed him. He died on the 17th, baby Patrice's birthday, and I didn't even know.' She set up a terrible wailing sound and the nurses had to come and tell her to be quiet.

That night she didn't even bother to feed Patrice. I lifted him from the cot and gave him the bottle the nurse brought. He snuggled into my arms, pulling on the teat vigorously. My breasts were sore. The milk had started to come in and I had to have them bound. His little fingers clasped mine and I smiled down at him. I had called my own baby John, but he was dead. Patrice was alive and making me smile, when I thought my heart had broken into a million tiny pieces.

I suppose that's why Gloria's words didn't sound outrageous when she woke me early the next morning. It was still dark in the ward and it took me a few moments to understand.

'I want you to look after Patrice, Frances,' she whispered. 'Francois needs me and it's no place for a baby at the moment. I know you'll be good to him. He was born on your baby's birthday. It won't be for long.'

Gloria and I didn't speak to each other for the rest of the day. It wasn't until the evening that I sat down on the chair by her bed.

I had made up my mind.

I didn't say anything to Harry. He'd only have kicked up a fuss. But a week after I returned from hospital, Gloria arrived in the middle of the afternoon with Patrice and all his paraphernalia. She would write, she said again and again, and she'd be back in six months at the most.

I made sure I fed the baby before Harry was due home, and I put everything out of sight in the front room. I cooked Harry his favourite steak and kidney pie for tea and waited.

'It's good to have you home, Frances girl,' he said as he scoffed the food. 'We'll be all right, just the two of us, you'll see.'

'Harry…' I busied myself at the sink so that he couldn't see my hands shaking, '…there's something I want to show you.'

'Go on, what have you bought now? I suppose you deserve a treat, what with, you know, the baby and all that.'

I went into the other room and picked up Patrice from the armchair where he was sleeping. I carried him into the kitchen where Harry was still eating.

'What the bleedin hell is that?' he shouted.

'A baby.'

'For gawd's sake, girl, I'm not blind! Whose baby is it, and when is it going home?'

I explained that Gloria had been called to a family emergency. She would only be gone a few days. 'She doesn't know anyone else.'

Harry's mouth opened. I stared at the yellow fur on his tongue, the broken tooth, while I braced myself for the roar of anger, the threatening fist. I shielded the baby's head. Mrs White, next door, didn't need to put her ear to the wall that day, nor for weeks to come. Harry raged and shouted, but I was determined.

It was a relief when he finally left. It was Patrice and me now.

I can't remember when I decided to call him Patrick. It was easier to say somehow. Gloria wrote every few days at first; then it dwindled to once a month. I had a photo of her which I showed Patrick from time to time. 'That's Mummy,' I would say. But after a while he used to point at me when he heard the word. I put the photo away between the leaves of the poetry book I'd received as a prize at school and hid it at the bottom of the drawer where I kept my mother's tablecloths. About a year after Harry left,

Gloria's letters dried up altogether. Patrick was mine.

We never had much money. I used to work at a dressmaker's and sometimes I had to leave Patrick on his own when I got the chance of overtime. I didn't really have friends I could ask. I didn't want people to get too close, asking questions. As far as anyone knew, I was looking after him for a time while his mother was away. I suppose we were an oddity, the two of us: my hair dead straight and red, his, frizzy; my skin pale and freckled, his, dark and shining. I know people used to point at us when we went out, but Patrick was such a beautiful child, you couldn't help but notice him.

The trouble started when he was about thirteen. I can still see the headmaster's face now.

'The thing is Mrs Harvey,' he began. 'Patrick's been drinking.'

I felt sweat creeping across my scalp. 'Whatever do you mean?' I asked in a much louder voice than I usually dared use.

'He's brought whisky into the playground and... worse than that...' he looked at me over his spectacles, 'he's encouraged other boys, I'm afraid.'

'I don't believe you. Patrick wouldn't do that.'

'Mrs Harvey, you must realise, this is very serious. I've got the safety of all the pupils to consider. If you could give me his mother's address...'

I stood up. 'I am his mother,' I said, straining every muscle so as not to cry.

I didn't believe it for one minute, but I had to ask Patrick just the same. He didn't even try to deny it. His face was closed and sulky looking, nothing like my beautiful son.

'I want you to promise you'll never do such a thing again.' I knew I had to be strong.

'I can't do that,' Patrick said.

It was the last honest thing he said to me for years.

*

'Another drink, Mum?' Patrick asks.

Frances looks up from the letter he's given her. She feels shy in front of this handsome stranger. So many hours imagining seeing him and now she can't think what to say.

'Have another drink,' he says again. 'What would you like?'

'Why are you here?' The question bursts from Frances's lips

22

like an over-full blister. She feels her cheeks redden. She wouldn't ask any questions, wouldn't make demands. That's what she told herself as she left home. And here she is, barely five minutes in his company and she says the very thing guaranteed to annoy him. She waits for the tantrum.

'I wanted to see you,' Patrick says. 'I thought it was about time I put things right between us.'

'Why now?'

'I've grown up.'

She gazes at his face, so different and yet so familiar. She remembers the softness of his baby skin, the warm musky smell of his damp hair after a bath. She fell in love with him the moment she first held him. Despite all the angry words, the rejection that followed, the love affair has never ended.

'It was hard, Mum,' Patrick begins. 'It wasn't just that I was black and different. I had to do whatever you said, be whoever you said.'

'I only wanted what was best for you.'

'What you thought was best. But I had to find out what I wanted. Who I was.'

Frances gulps back her drink. 'Do you hate me?' she asks.

'Hate you?' He takes her hand. 'I owe everything to you.'

'Oh Patrick.'

'My name's Patrice,' he says softly.

Frances stays in the bar long after Patrick has gone. She orders a bowl of pasta and another drink. She bends over the letter she's read countless times already. It is from Gloria.

'My dear friend,

'How can I ever thank you for taking care of our beloved boy so well? You have done a marvellous job. Patrice has told me it wasn't easy for you.

'His father would be proud of him. He was killed in the war of independence, so Patrice will never know him. But he's seen photos and I've told him what a wonderful man he was.

'Perhaps one day when you come over here to visit Patrice I will explain why I never returned to England as I promised. It was very difficult. But I could never have been as good a mother as you have been and I thank you from the bottom of my heart.

Gloria.'

'What, you still here?'

Frances glances up. The young blond man with the nose ring is looking down at her.

'I forgot my wallet,' he explains. 'Has your son gone?'

'Yes, he had to meet someone. But he's coming to see me tomorrow. And he's invited me for a holiday in Jamaica. He lives there, you see.' Frances has never said so much to a stranger. 'I wanted to ask you,' she goes on, feeling bolder by the moment. 'Does the ring in your nose hurt?'

'Yeah, it's a pain.'

'Why do you keep it?'

'My Mum hates it, and I can't let her think she's won, can I? See you.'

Aisling Tempany

Why not to take cynical people for a walk round West-Kennet Long Barrow

'If you stop to think about it
Most of England has been someone's grave
After all, this country is so small.

So when you've been dead for a very long time
It's no matter if your body is dug up
For a museum display, while your primitive chamber

Might form part of some pretty country walk.
One for intellectual tourists or privileged pagans
Always searching for their roots in nature.'

Academic Poet

Academic poet
He knows how good he is.
His students buy his books
And come to him for signatures.

Academic poet
Has a privileged position.
He lives on a university income
With an office and research leave.

Academic poet
Writes a three page poem for his dick
And connects it to a national tradition.
He doesn't write smut, he writes culture.

Academic poet
Puts himself in a poetic tradition
Connected to Eliot and Hughes
He improves their poetic sequences.

Academic Poet
Whose work is so outstanding
Still works mainly as an academic
Not purely as a poet.

Isabella Mead

The Fens

It is as if a film of it
is paused by the remote; the distant screen
stammering and glazed, the channel abandoned.

So stuck like that, seasons do not rush in
with accidents of rain or dispersals of sun.
Gulls swell and are stilled with the clouds.

Or in the middle of nowhere a GNER train
heaves to a standstill and in the pause
between the muffled stop and resigned announcement

misted condensation clears on the windows
and only slightly adjusts itself to blend
into the massive grey sky beyond

blotted at an edge by Ely Cathedral
and filled with marshes, towering grasses
and solid pools. No one moves across the occasions of land

though, testing the ground, would find that it gives
only by centimetres, and sink so far
as barely to fringe the frozen reflections.

The channel is flicked; the train moves on.
Surfers and passengers bypass the breadth
of the grasses and pools in muted tones

and never move in to colour the monochrome,
unlock the marshland, untie the sky;
the pools are loopholes to latch onto.

Julie Mellor

Rabbits

He would skin them in the kitchen,
lift them by their feet like newborns,
drape their dead weight onto last week's
newspaper. The knife sang on the whetstone
as he teased the blade sharp,
the barbershop movement of his hand
back and forth under the strip light.

I stood in the corner, dared myself to watch
as he made the first cut, peeled back a lip
of skin on the abdomen and began to work
the rabbit free of itself, easing
the cleavered leg stumps through cuffs of fur,
the way he prised me out of my duffel coat
when I was numb from playing in the snow.

The smell of intestines filled the room,
sour as rising dough, and behind the door
the dog frisked the skirting board, whining
at the scent of blood. Stripped of its skin,
the rabbit gleamed, purple-grey. I longed
to run my fingers across its veiled ribs,
touch the cavity where its heart had been.

My Father Winds the Grandfather Clock

turns the brass key to open the case,
catches the pendulum by the throat,
stills it with his roughened hand,
then feeds the weights
upwards on their brass chains

to their starting point a week ago.
Every Saturday morning
he performs this act, stopping time,
adding seconds, minutes,

to the span of his life.

Thud
Rosemary Mairs

She watched the men as they fed the hens. One of them, the taller one, made a clucking noise with his tongue, throwing grain and scraps of food in wide arcs. The smaller man quickly emptied his bucket, and started collecting eggs. He knew where to look; among particular clumps of long grass, under a bush.

They weren't dressed like farmers; both wore worn, faded raincoats and trousers that were too short, even the small man's. It was their shoes that gave them away; farmers didn't wear white plimsolls.

The tall man watched the birds squawking and fighting over the food, before also collecting eggs. He did it slowly, examining each one carefully, then placing it in his bucket. Was he looking at their size; colour? He stood still, looking vacantly around, as though he'd forgotten what he was in the act of doing. The other man walked over, putting a hand on his arm, and he started collecting again.

Sarah stepped forward from behind the hen shed. One of them saw her, then the other. They stared; she stared, like two species of animal encountering each other for the first time.

'Hello,' she said, lifting her hand in a half-wave.

She took another step forward. 'I hope you don't mind...' She cleared her throat. 'They gave me directions in the village.'

The taller of the two men turned away, looking for eggs again. The other held out his bucket in her direction. 'What have you for us?'

It took a moment for Sarah to work out what he meant. 'No, I don't want eggs. I'm not here to barter.'

She moved closer to the man. His face was lined and weather beaten; it was difficult to judge his age. She guessed around fifty.

'I'm a journalist. Can I ask you a few questions? I'm doing a feature on alternative lifestyles. You guys are just what I'm looking for.'

The taller man came over. His bucket was full to the brim with eggs. He looked down at the eggs as he spoke. 'What you give us?'

Sarah had to explain again. 'No, I'm not here to barter. Although, that's one of the things I want to ask you about. If you could give me a few minutes of your time, I…'

The last words were spoken to the men's backs as they walked away from her. Sarah followed them, her shoes catching on the rough stones underfoot. Dilapidated sheds with tin roofs lined each side of the yard through which she walked behind them. She noticed the careful way the men held the buckets of eggs to stop them spilling out. They reached a shed at the top of the yard, and the taller man opened the door, disappearing inside. The small man lifted eggs out of his bucket, cleaning them with a cloth.

'I'm Sarah, by the way.' When she got no response she went on, 'I'll pay you for an interview.'

The tall man reappeared out of the shed, leaving the door open behind him.

'So, what do you keep in here?' Sarah asked, looking through the open door for sign of an animal. At the far side of the shed was what looked like an electric cooker. A fridge against another wall was also rusted brown. On a table were mugs and plates. Beside it was a door in the wall.

She turned back to the men. They were hunkered down beside the buckets of eggs, cleaning them, then filling cardboard cartons with six eggs each. The tall man looked up, gazing at the yard beyond Sarah, before looking down again, as though remembering what he was doing. His eyes were an unusual colour—grey flecked with green.

'I believe you're brothers.'

This was one of the few things that people in the village knew about them. They didn't lift their heads from their work.

Once the egg boxes were filled, the tall man placed them carefully inside plastic bags, and the brothers carried them across the yard.

Sarah followed. They made their way down a narrow, overgrown lane and onto the road where Sarah had left her car.

'Can I give you a lift, guys? Are you going to the village?'

They didn't turn their heads, walking past her car.

'Do you mind if I tag along?' she asked. The small man glanced back at her, but didn't speak.

She had to walk quickly to keep up with them. The tall man had a limp; she'd noticed it earlier, and it got more pronounced now as the journey continued. The small brother took short, quick strides, glancing back at her again as they rounded a bend in the road. Little and Lame. Well, she had to call them something.

She watched the backs of the two men walking in front of her. Lame was round-shouldered. How did someone with a limp move so quickly?

Sarah walked faster, closing the gap between them. 'They told me in the village that one of you used to be a car mechanic.'

Little's step faltered. So it was him. Lame looked anxiously at his brother. Her words had upset them both. They would know she was lying, that she didn't hear this information in the village. They increased their pace, trying to leave her behind. Her heels clicked faster on the road, keeping up with them.

They reached the village. Lame opened the door of the only shop, the one in which Sarah had asked directions. The man behind the counter nodded at Lame as he set the bags of eggs onto the counter. The brothers collected some things from the shelves—bread, cheese, tea bags, a few tins. The strain of Sarah's presence showed in the hurried, jerky movements of their hands. The man at the counter put their groceries in the bags that the eggs had been in, nodding again to the brothers.

Sarah followed them back along the road. 'So, what now guys? This is really good of you, letting me hang out with you.'

They walked quicker, and she let them leave her behind. When she reached her car they were no longer in sight. She opened the door, sitting inside, leaning her head back against the head rest and closing her eyes. She had to decide what to do, now that the search was over.

Now that she had found him.

The yard was silent. The door into the shed in which they lived was still lying open, the way they had left it when they took the eggs to the village. Sarah stepped inside. It didn't smell bad, the way she expected it to, just damp. A cooker, a fridge, a table, two chairs, some crockery, that was it. There was no sink in the small room. The concrete floor was swept clean. Sarah walked towards the door in the wall opposite.

'Hello?'

She waited.

She put her hand on the door handle, opening it.

It took a moment for her eyes to adjust to the dim light. There was no one inside. A bed lined each wall of the tiny room, with blankets folded neatly on top. The only light was from a window about a foot square.

Outside again, Sarah opened the doors of the other sheds. One contained farm implements—wheelbarrows, spades, buckets. The next door she opened gave her a start, even though she had been expecting to find an animal.

The cow turned its head in her direction, also startled. She almost laughed, because their lifestyle was so predictable. It seemed well cared for; clean straw was piled thickly on the floor. Its black hide was gleaming. It annoyed her that it was well looked after.

She opened the shed door wider, standing back out of sight in the yard. The cow walked out past her. She shut the door behind it, waving her arms at it, and it walked across the yard, towards the lane. She chased after it, waving her arms again and it broke into a gallop down the lane, disappearing out of sight.

Sarah burst out laughing; she couldn't help herself. When it subsided, she stood still, listening.

What was that noise?

She walked in the direction of it, behind the shed in which they lived. She could see the brothers now; they were in a small field. Lame was knocking a wooden post into the ground. Little was on his knees among drills of vegetables.

'Hello again. A vegetable garden; I might have known. You guys are really self-sufficient.'

She walked along the first drill. 'I've been having a look in the sheds. I see you've got a cow. You really do have the good life here… I don't think much of your living accommodation though. Your bedroom's like a prison cell.'

She made her way along the second drill, stopping beside Little. 'If I was a journalist, which I'm not, I don't think my readers would be impressed by your lifestyle.'

He kept his back to her. She hunkered down beside him, her fingers lifting green stalks growing from the soil. 'So, what's this?'

She pulled on the stalks, bringing up something. 'Oh, it's an onion… Well, it will be when it's grown.'

She tossed it to the side, walking along the drill, pulling them up as she went. She threw the half-grown vegetables in Little's direction. One of them hit him on the back.

'Oh, look! I got a bigger one.' She walked towards Lame, holding it up for him to see. 'Not big enough to eat, though,' and she tossed it away.

Lame tied netting to the post that he had hammered into the

ground. She moved closer to him. 'Have you worked out who I am yet?'

He kept his face turned away from her, his fingers fumbling with the netting.

She gazed down at the area of vegetables beside him. 'I know what these are.' She fingered the leafy stalks, pulling on one. A carrot, the size of her finger came up. 'Yes, I thought so. So tiny though.' She threw it to the side, pulling up the one beside it, then the next one.

Lame walked away, breaking into a run, heading towards the yard. Little watched him.

'I have to admire your loyalty.' Sarah made her way over to Little. 'But is he worth it, do you think? And where does your loyalty draw a line? What if he'd murdered someone for example, what if that had been his crime, instead of...'

She was close to Little now. 'Would you still have stuck by him then?'

She moved even closer. 'You know who I am, don't you?'

He stared back at her. 'What do you want?'

Sarah wanted to shout, I want him to pay for what he did. She wanted to scream it at him, but instead she said, 'I want to know why you stick by him. You had a job... a house.'

'He's my brother.'

'But...'

'I look after him.'

He turned away from her, walking towards the yard. Some of the vegetables Sarah had pulled up were lying in his path and he picked them up as he went. They would laugh about her later, at the silly girl who thought she could intimidate them by destroying a few onions.

She picked up a spade lying on the ground beside her. Little heard her footstep behind him, glancing back. The spade caught him on the side of the head. He fell forward.

She hadn't hit him hard. He would get up. Any minute now he would sit up. His face was to the side; his eyes closed. She hunkered down beside him; watching, listening. His breathing was short and laboured.

Thud... thud.

Sarah glanced up, listening to the noise, trying to work out what it was. She took one last look at Little before standing up.

34

She had to focus on what she had come for.

Thud... thud.

She walked towards the yard in the direction of the thudding noise. Lame was chopping logs on a block of wood. There was a neat pile of sticks on the ground beside him.

Sarah leant against a shed wall, watching him. He chopped each log in two on the block, raising the axe above his head, then into two again, until they were split into small sticks.

The pile got higher.

'Do you barter firewood at the shop?'

When he didn't reply she repeated, 'Do you exchange these for food at the shop, David?'

He showed no emotion when she said his name, but she could see that his hand was trembling as he picked up another log, placing it on the block.

Thud... thud

He suited Lame better anyway.

'Do they know in the village that they have a rapist living among them?'

Thud... thud... thud.

'What was it like in prison?'

Thud... thud

'Do you think I look like my mother?'

He picked up another log, carefully placing it on the block, his eyes concentrated on it, as if Sarah wasn't there.

Thud... thud.

'I think they have a right to know, in the village.' She moved forward, walking towards him. 'Do you want to tell them, or will I?'

The split log fell to the ground. He picked up one half, replacing it on the block, focusing on it as though his life depended on it. He swung the axe.

Thud... thud.

She was just a few feet away from him, 'Do you still see her face? Do you still hear her scream?'

Thud... His arm paused in the motion of lifting the axe; his eyes, the same colour as hers, focused on her face.

It was a threat, but she didn't move.

Something in his eyes changed, and then with one hand he swung the axe.

Thud...

He didn't yell or scream. The log in his other hand on the block turned red. Her eyes blinked closed, but she had to look at it, at the meat-raw flesh and sinew of what was left of his hand.

She turned, running down the lane to her car. He still hadn't made a sound, and as she drove away she opened her mouth and the noise that came out sounded inhuman, animal-like. Was this how her mother had screamed?

This was what she had wanted, wasn't it, for him to be punished properly? This was what she wanted.

She pressed down on the accelerator, trying to get away from the noise in the car, from the noise in her head that never went away.

She pressed harder. The next bend of the road appeared. His hand for what he'd done—a barter, an exchange, think of it like that. The noise in her head intensified, pressing against her skull.

The car reached the bend.

Thud… the wheel span out of her hands. The car began turning, spinning; once, twice. She had never believed it when people said their entire lives flashed before them in just seconds, but hers was now; he would be the end of it, his hand—

Instead, vacant grey eyes, flecked with green; her mother's voice, 'He didn't know what he was doing, Sarah. He wasn't right…'

Thud—the car hit the dyke again, finally stopping.

Sarah sat very still, her arm throbbing from when she'd been flung against the door as the car was spinning. The buzzing in her head was gone, but it would start again any second now. 'Didn't know what he was doing.' She kept saying it out loud, over and over; 'Didn't know what he was doing,' reaching into her pocket for her mobile, pressing the numbers.

'Ambulance… There's been an accident. His hand… He needs an ambulance.'

Jacci Bulman

a call to say if you have something terrible

In the midst of all this middling
playing at getting life correct
I spend the afternoon waiting
for a phone call

that could jerk us into another kind
of everything: where jam tastes different;
putting your wellies by the door
means something else.
Where planning a holiday in summer
becomes some fantasy game.

So now the rest of the day is like scenery
out the window of a stilted time-machine.
It's hurtling past
lines merging slowly into a glaze
that almost hurts the mind.

Meanwhile the machine feels no gravity
no wind on the face.
Only a sense of separated matter.

Patrick Lodge

The East Yorkshire Crematorium
for G.R.

No God brought you to this place. The weave
unravelled: spun, measured and cut. Now each
standing at the lectern thumbs a thin thread
teasing for meaning back to the entwining knot.
Outside, the west wind pipes up the escarpment,
the shielding poplar line shivers; a silver
leaf mantilla drapes the black comb of trunks.
Eloquently, a calliope wheezing an old-time hymn,
the trees lament their bending. Through stained glass
I watch a crow court squawking sky secrets;
lifting from twisted thorn nests, woven tight
to the tree scaffold, they hang, between earth and cloud,
wings stiff, waiting on a wish to be made. Cras! Cras!
They clack their hollow hope. There is no future
beyond this building; a one-way valve, the heat
plume shimmering high into empty, weightless air.

Trisagion
Thrice holy

I

Tiresias the seer comes towards me,
Stands in sun-faded red flowered dress,
Transparent bag stuffed
With gleanings of street and shore.
He holds out a present of driftwood
Bleached and salty, entwined like albino snakes.
Tells me what the birds have said today,
In couplets I cannot understand;
Reclaiming this temple mound from saints and sinners,
He dances off.

II

In the Café Caryatids an old man rests,
Blue painted chair tilted in the doorway.
He sat there yesterday, will be there tomorrow.
Teeth and pullover holed and brown, he stares
Mute at the road, a drone of tourists passing.
Bacchants and satyrs they follow the umbrella thyrsos
Snake through café chairs and shop front T-shirts,
Short-stepping in rhythm after a guide; yellow tights,
Black ankle boots, she is a queen,
Finding honey in the columns and slabs
Littering the temple site of Apollo; the residue,
A carved henge, faces westwards, leads nowhere
Now, admits to nothing; a lizard's eye
Unblinking red, through which
Shutters click and cameras flash; the moment
When light folds into darkness remains elusive.

III

The kouros at Apollonas reclines obtuse against the hillside,
breathes out asphodels in wave-froth to the edge of the cliff.
Tourists climb and slither in search of the shot
To validate memory's convivial hyperbole.
Unrealised Dionysus, a marble moraine,
A black smudge against the darker quarry wall,
Suffers them; but dreams of standing free of this rock umbilical—
The headland a plinth floating between sea and bluer sky,
Arms raised in welcome to sail and oar.
When the gods went, villagers dropped hammers,
Stopped chipping against the hard grain and
Returned to their goats and groves—their piss-poor soil.
Those terraces, tribal scars cut into the mountain-sides,
In turn abandoned for easier fleeces each Summer boat disgorged;
A new mythology of excess is today's orthodoxy.
Dionysus, be content to lie, weeping ferns into the pockmark pools.

David Gill

The Space before the House

All day spent in summer's mess
Clearing the convivial.
Our breezy, lidless salon cools
Beside the conifers and balding vines,
The terrace steps and firewood and sky.
Pouring rain from candles' cratered cream.
Unbolting gleaming joints in table hips
Then oiling every limb.

Among the tangled colonies of home —
The gaps we leave — this place is mostly mine:
The barbecues and breakfasts out;
The wish to sit in stars.

October's ivy sprays are cut.
Pots of craning flower death,
One head in ten still bright,
Are wheeled away. The chairs
Which marked the oblong of our meals
Are stacked inside to dry.
Staying out: a loop of lights;
The hanging griddles' greasy feast.
A box of soil set in flags
Is weeded of its tired leaves.
Herbs are trimmed. By afternoon
There is a space before the house.
An emptiness not seen since March,
Where winter months can stay
And squeeze their coldness into bricks.
Days fail from three, and long for spring.
As many springs as you would want
To spend beyond the kitchen wall,
And sometimes sit and gaze
As if the warmth will never leave.

Drying Wood

Against a summer wall.

Snug circles facing south
And stacked to form a square.

The resinous bleed amber beads
And jewel each circumference.

The rest will crack to death.
Slow, sunny, further deaths

Where seasons' sleeping flaws converge
By splitting every cylinder.

Their lightless fissures sketch
Distorted winter stars

In lines as thin and cold

As nights when they will burn.

Monster under the bed
Lezanne Clannachan

Eddie pulls up his hood and rests his head on the back of the bench. Above him, the glass ceiling of Waterloo station soars away. The space makes him dizzy. Feels like he's inside a giant hot-air balloon flying close to the sun.

Something hits his lap. Lifting his head, he comes face to face with a panting dog, its front paws pattering about on his legs.

'Hey boy.' The dog licks his wrists as he rubs its ears. It's a mongrel. Looks a little like his Beanie. Its owner is carrying a stained, green sleeping bag over one shoulder. His boots are stuffed with bits of newspaper like birds' nests.

Some of his classmates would probably have given the man a hard time, shouted a bit of abuse. They don't like what they don't know. But Eddie's sick of what he knows. He asks, 'What's your dog's name?'

The man ignores him, pulling on the dog's leash. 'Get down, you daft buggar.'

'I don't mind.' Eddie sits forward to stroke the dog, which jumps back on his lap. He hugs it, his face in its fur. It even smells like Beanie after she's been fetching sticks from the river.

'Get off my dog,' the man says. He won't meet Eddie's eye, but his face is all creased up with anger. 'You leave my dog alone.'

Eddie pushes the dog gently from his lap. The man yanks it to his side so hard it whimpers and Eddie feels bad. He wants to call after the man, saying he didn't mean any harm. He misses his own dog, that's all.

Leaning back again, Eddie puts a hand on the white box by his side. Just checking it's there. His stomach rumbles and he can't resist opening the lid. Hot sugar and raisins. Six Eccles cakes that cost him almost twenty quid. Closing the lid, he frets again about the bakery logo - Hampstead Baker's House. It's not the place his mother talks about from her childhood. That one no longer exists. He wasted hours looking for it. Now he'll be late home.

'May I?' A woman stops by his bench.

He puts the box on his lap; pushes his hood off his head.

She smiles as she sits down. 'This is my bench, you know.'

'Didn't see your name on it,' Eddie says.

She laughs at his bad joke, the light catching a diamond piercing above her lip. She's wearing a lot of make-up. Trying to look younger than she is. Like his mum, so careful with her make-up every morning. What's the point? he thinks when he's feeling mean.

'This one yours?' She asks as a train slides into the platform.

He shakes his head, having memorised the timetable last night. Not many trains stop at Frenley. Closing his eyes, he listens to the footfall of passengers, like an avalanche of rocks down a mountain. It's the noise he hadn't been prepared for—traffic, sirens, roadworks and underneath it, the great roar of the city.

'Been to college?'

'Shopping. First time in London.' Despite weeks of planning and pleading with his mum—just pretend I'm at school—he'd woken up nervous. That's when he realised how easy it could be to close your front door and never leave.

'I'm Angie, by the way.'

'Eddie.' He shakes her hand with a firm grip to show strength of character. It's manners not money that matter, his mum liked to say when he was little.

The woman leans in, tapping the box. 'What you got?'

'Eccles cakes.'

'My fave.'

'My mum's too. It's her birthday present.' The word 'mum' makes an anxious bubble in his stomach. The platform clock tells him he's missed her tea. He pictures her on the edge of the sofa, nervous as a bird, wanting to go into the kitchen to make toast, but unable to. 'I should be home by now.'

'Strict is she, your mum?'

Eddie shakes his head. 'She's not well. She needs me.'

'It's nice to be needed. My two only want me for wiping bums and making lunch boxes.'

'You don't look like a mum.'

She laughs. 'Nicest thing anyone has said to me all day. All week.' Resting her arm on the back of the bench, she tilts her head against her hand. 'So, what about you? Do you have a girlfriend?'

Eddie's face gets hot.

'Made you blush,' the woman says. She thinks it's shyness, but she's wrong. It's anger and it catches him off guard. He makes himself remember the grateful look on his mum's face when he fetches her rug, brushes her hair, rubs her feet. What would I do without you, my boy? His anger shames him.

'Plenty of time for all that.' Angie taps her feet on the floor. 'Bloody train's always late.'

Eddie looks up. It's starting to get dark. The evening sky pushes the glass ceiling towards him, the vast hangar space no longer taking his breath away. He thinks about Beanie. And Lucy with her long, straight hair.

Angie doesn't try to speak to him again as they wait for the train, but when it arrives she gives his knee a shake. 'Aren't you going to get on?'

'I'll get the next one.' The anger sits on his chest like a fat, ugly toad. If he goes home feeling like this, it'll ruin his mum's birthday surprise. Angie looks like she has something to say; he pretends to watch a group of girls in short skirts and stupid-looking shoes until she turns away.

When the platform is empty once more, he straightens. Realises he's crushed the neat edges of the pastry box. The train curves away with the tracks until he loses it in the dark.

What was he thinking, letting it go? His mum will have finished the flask of coffee and tuna sandwiches ages ago. Worse still, she'll be peeking through the gaps in the curtains, wondering where he is. He can't even call her. She got rid of the telephone years ago. He closes his eyes, holding the cakes.

Do you remember the monster under your bed? It's how his mum explained it to him once. You know it's not real, but that doesn't stop the fear. Even now he remembers jumping from the chest of drawers onto his bed so the monster couldn't grab his ankles.

Footsteps along the quiet platform. He doesn't bother to open his eyes. What's there to be scared of? A mugger? An unfriendly man with a dog? So what. So what.

'The next train isn't for an hour.' Angie is standing with her hands crossed in front of her like a sorry child. 'Thought you might like some company.'

'What about your kids?'

'At my folks. I usually do overtime on Thursdays.' She shrugs. 'No-one's interested in insurance at the moment.' When he doesn't answer, she takes a breath and says, 'I got on the train. Found a window seat and all. Then I saw you sitting there, looking lost.'

'I'm not.' The anger's fading. He never meets new people, hardly sees those he knows. His world is shrinking. Perhaps his mum's illness is contagious after all.

'I felt bad for teasing you earlier.'

Eddie shrugs, opens the box and chooses a cake. Takes a huge bite, holding the pastries out to Angie.

'I shouldn't,' she says, taking one.

'How old are you?' he asks.

'Older than your big sister—if you have one—and younger than your mum. You?'

'Fifteen.' He finishes the cake in three bites, licks sugar crystals off his fingers.

'You look older,' she says.

'I know.'

Angie touches his arm as he takes another Eccles. 'What about your mum?'

'I had a girlfriend once,' he says through his mouthful. 'And a dog.'

She's sitting very still. Like adults do when they're scared of saying something that might make you shut up. 'Last Saturday my mum asked me to take my dog to Blackdown—this massive forest close to where we live.'

Beanie leaping, wagging her tail as he looped the rope through her collar; thinking it was a game. Love you, Beanie.

'I tied her to a tree and walked away.' What he doesn't say is how long he crouched behind a bush listening to his dog calling for him. Biting his thumb knuckle so he wouldn't cry.

Angie frowns. 'Why would she make you do that?'

'She's scared of anything I might love more than her.' He feels bad about saying it, even though it's true.

'I don't get it.' She picks at the diamond above her lip. 'You could have said no.'

That's what they all say. Mac and the rest of the gang said the same thing when he stopped football practice. Even Lucy. After everything he told her.

'Is that what happened to your girlfriend?'

'Nah. We wanted to go to the cinema, but Lucy didn't fancy the bus because it was raining. She said, "Can't you get your mum to give us a lift?" She started saying dumb things like that.'

They sit in silence, neither of them moving as another train arrives. Angie says, 'The next one is the last.'

46

'I know.' After he bought the pastries, he'd walked and walked; just for the pleasure of one road leading to another. Home, with its drawn curtains and closed up smell far away.

'What's wrong with your mum?'

He answers because he'll never see Angie again. 'First she stopped going out with her mate Lilian. Then she wouldn't visit the neighbours. For my eleventh birthday she promised to take me to the cinema. She stood for ages with the front door open. In the end she gave up and lay down on the sofa and I took Beanie for a walk. After that she couldn't even go into the garden.'

'And your dad?'

'Got sick of looking after her.'

He doesn't ask about Angie's life though he supposes he should. He's not sure what she wants. A lost puppy perhaps. He offers her the last pastry. She looks worried, shaking her head. 'You *will* get the next train, right?'

'Of course.' What if he doesn't? He plays it out like a film in his head. Ticket barrier, neon concourse, London road. He'd walk. That's what he'd do. Until his legs ached and his head was clear. The idea catches hold of him like a fever. Leaning over the arm of the bench, he vomits up his mum's Eccles cakes.

'Christ.' Angie leaps up, hesitates, then fusses over him like a fly. 'The thing is, Eddie, when I saw you sitting there, you looked just like my little brother.'

He wipes his mouth. 'Good looking bloke, then.'

She doesn't smile. 'Bit taller than you, I'd say. It's more a feeling I got when I saw you.'

All the girls feel that way, he wants to say because she's looking so serious.

'He ran away when he was about your age,' Angie says.

Eddie pictures himself walking out of the station into the huge London night. 'What happened to him?'

'He came back a week later, but he wasn't really the same old Jamie.'

'Why not?'

'It's not like something bad happened.' Angie plucks at her diamond stud again. 'Turns out he'd been sleeping on a mate's floor.'

'But he came home.' Eddie slides down to rest his head again. 'Happy ending.'

'He never *properly* came back. We spent all our time waiting for

47

him to disappear again.'

They hear the last train approaching at the same time. Angie tries to pull him to his feet. 'Home time.'

Eddie shrugs her off.

She presses the door button, rushes back to get him. 'What are you waiting for?'

'Have you noticed how scared everyone is?' Eddie says. 'Some homeless man thinks I'm going to take his dog. You're worried I won't get on the train. My mum's terrified of her own life.' And he, himself, maybe most of all; scared of becoming scared.

'I have to get on,' Angie keeps saying and finally she does.

When he was eight, he crawled under his bed, lay on the dusty carpet until he knew—felt it in his bones—there was no monster. If he doesn't come home, his mum will have to leave the house. Even if she only gets as far as the garden gate.

The doors close. He can see Angie by the window. She won't look at him. As the train gathers speed, his heart starts pumping as if he's running to catch it. He leaves the empty pastry box on the bench and walks—one step after another—towards the ticket barrier.

4343

Sue Moules

Oak Woods

Blue sky above green leaves
shadowed light
on the woodland path,
buttercup bright.

Back through the decades
to a century before,
these trees, old as earth,
survive and thrive.

From acorns cupped in green
this wood where cows graze,
acorns hoofed in, deep in mud,
for future trees.

The glass of river
pours over rocks,
boulders of time
sealed in sediment.

Claire Dyer

In the hat I wear shopping
Portrait of Frau P. in the South (Paul Klee 1879 – 1940)

He chose to paint me in orange;
hard, burnt brushings, tinged
with moss and charcoal
and black. He made my eyes
conceptual, in the hope
I could not see you judge me
in the hat I wear shopping,
or see you see the heart he drew in
below the imperceptible bump
of my breasts, or the mouth
etched at half-tilt so my words
fall at angles, so easily unheard.
He saw me distorted,
fairground-reflection-bent, *sans* hands,
sans ears so I cannot touch you
or hear you. And I will always wonder
if, perhaps, I took off
the hat I wear shopping
and he took the mirror away,
I could be unviolated,
unstolen, whole again.

Exhibition piece

He probably wore gloves, his tool belt
creased in familiar folds, weighted
just so with Stanley knife, spare blades.

He may have just eaten; ham and cheese
on white, left by his wife's cross hands on
the table in the hall — tin foil

a silver sound when unwrapped,
and he probably would stand back
to check his work — frame

spirit-level flat; the landscape a ploughed
field, horses' heads bent low, sky massive
and unafraid, and he would remember

back to the small thread of a skylark song,
himself a boy with heat in his hair,
his grandfather's farm-tired smile in his hands.

Photograph, 1959

My mother's hands are at rest
on the tabletop; she is
a still-life of cigarette smoke and satin.
She is smiling, has eleven years to go.

To her right my father's
hopeful head bends to listen. He is
slender, cradles me as a spark
somewhere between his pocket and his eye.

My hands hold the photograph;
are the hands my mother's
would have been had they grown
old; they conjure on keyboards

and in kitchens, rarely rest,
knit chronicles with veins and bones,
with scars; they are her testament,
her album, her frame.

Marcus Smith

Sitting for a Moment

In the long late heat of a summer afternoon
when time has forgotten its daily go-rounds
and the park I pass most days echoes the calls
of hungry birds and children running barefoot,
the sky feels as light as the moon, which has ventured out
for sun and company, and I hear a deep crackle
on the branch above, and loosened in my chest
a sudden conscious breaking urge
to hike the green mountain in the near distance
or simply stay rooted here by a flowering tree
while the sun vanishes and stars congregate.
Sharing in that great fact until dawn,
I watch the whole known mystery start again
as now an ant, taking the time it needs, explores
the veins of a leaf on the grass and the veins of my hands.

Driving with My Daughter

We are moving quickly, much too quickly
to focus on the illusion of rushing lands
you survey with the keenness of an animal.
Are you studying the horizon for an end?
Do the geese flying overhead startle you
with their noisy freedom? Will how they stay
close together in the immense sky scare you
as much as the seriousness in your eyes
(brown as fallow fields are vast and empty)
frighten me with fallow recollection
of all the times I have traveled alone.
Now comes the mystery of powerlines.
Now an airplane roars, soars and disappears.
Now a freight train rattles through wheat fields,
Thumping in my heart, grinding through my belly.

In the mountains it was trees and more trees
a blur called forest. By the shining sea
wave after wave, no end or beginning.
Now you ask why so many streets and houses,
ask, "What's this place?" as if you've always felt,
without your innocence knowing it knows,
how easy it suddenly is to feel lost
in a familiar place while somewhere ahead,
foreign as ancient maps, must be the home
you, like me, peering into the rear view
of fogged mirrors, may have to give up finding.

Space
Ayesha Heble

Madge was convinced that Uma had been hiding certain things of hers. Earlier it had been kitchen things—one out of a set of six blue mugs, which rather ruined the set, the sharper kitchen knife, a plastic Tidy Susan which she had specially bought to separate her chopped vegetables for when she made a stir-fry—little things like that. But this time it was just too bad, she couldn't find her black trousers anywhere, even though she was certain she had taken them off the line herself and kept them in the spare bedroom for Uma to iron. Of course, she could wear the other black pair, but the material was some synthetic stuff that made her perspire behind the knees. Madge vowed to speak to Uma about it when she next came in; it was just too bad.

Sometimes the things turned up eventually, or disappeared altogether, depending on how much of a fuss she made. Uma would swear blind that she hadn't kept them where they would eventually be found, and it was Madam herself who must have put them there. And of course, Madge could never be sure. How else had the kitchen knife eventually found its way to the bathroom cabinet—unless, she had tried to use it to pry open the bathroom window—unsuccessfully, as it turned out. Or the Tidy Susan under her bed, with newspaper cuttings in each separate compartment—a rough and ready filing system when she found an interesting item while reading the newspaper on her bedroom veranda. The blue mug she never found.

The trouble was that the flat was too small. In the five and a half years she had been employed at this university in a country as far away from her own as she could get, she had collected a veritable treasure house of things—things that had memories attached to them, things that might come in useful some day, things that you never knew what use you might find for. She had collected plants in pots, hangings on the wall, rugs on the floor, printed throws over the sofa, cushions within its folds, a wind chime in front of the window, a lamp stand behind the armchair, spare towels inside the drawers and a welcome mat outside the front door—every preposition of place that could relate one object to another was represented. It probably came of being a teacher of English for too long.

And books, of course. There were books everywhere—the bookshelves provided by the University had long since declared themselves hopelessly inadequate to the task of housing her vast library, which had now to be accommodated in various ways not always suitable to their standing. So it was that the *Rubayat of Omar Khayyam* found itself on the shelf in the bathroom, next to T.S. Eliot's *Cats* and *The Nine Parts of Desire* by Geraldine Brooks. Shakespeare's *Complete Works* found itself in her kitchen and *Thai Cooking Made Easy* in the study. The dining room, which also doubled as her music room, had mainly her sheets of music and biographies of composers, though if one looked closely one might also find a book on *Keeping Indoor Plants*. Her bedside table was reserved for books that she happened to be reading at that particular time, but since she tended to read two or three simultaneously—one in the daytime and another just before going to bed, and maybe a third when she didn't feel like either one or the other—that was crowded as well. There were also piles of books on the floor, next to the bed, next to the dressing table, next to the desk, as well as on the bed, on the dressing table and on the desk. She planned to catalogue them all one day, and arrange them either alphabetically according to author, or categorically according to subject. But she hadn't got round to it.

Just as she hadn't got round to cutting out the articles from the newspapers that she collected for that purpose. They would make such good material for her writing class—authentic text for the students to analyze and work on. The articles that she *had* got round to cutting out were kept in the Tidy Susan until a better filing system could be found for them. It was a rough and ready system, but it worked. Most of the time, anyway. Her students loved her classes, and learned to look at words in entirely new ways and find meanings beyond the words in how they were put together, or even sometimes, in how they were arranged on the page. They learned about the power that came from words and being able to use words in certain ways. They learned that writing was a process and not a product, that one could play around with words and say the same thing in many different ways. Even if you were a second language learner.

Madge also had dreams, hidden away among her potted plants and piles of books. Dreams of going to far-off lands and of coming back home, dreams of becoming famous as a writer rather than a teacher of writing, dreams even of finding that one person who would help her make some sense of it all. Preferably, but not necessarily, a man. Which, face it, was not particularly likely at her age. It might have been, at one time, when she had first come to this place, so far away from her own home. But not far enough because eventually you brought everything down to your level, and even the most exotic became routine. And so her dreams of far-off lands still remained unfulfilled, even though she took every opportunity of travelling during the semester breaks to places with the most exotic of names. Egypt, Lebanon, Madagascar, Zanzibar. But when she came back her dreams of far-away places had receded even further away, further out of reach.

As had her dreams of finding the preferably but not necessarily man. There had been that one amazing classmate when she had been a student herself, in *the* sixties, as opposed to *her* sixties, whom she had shared a flat and so many discussions with, whom she had rather fancied but who had eventually turned out to be gay—wasn't that just predictable! And so here she was with her virginity and her dreams intact, but not particularly bothered any longer by their presence. Most of her friends these days tended to be women anyway, and they went quite a long way in filling up the spaces inside.

Her dreams of becoming a writer—ah, now that was something else! That *did* bother her—the fact that ex-colleagues had now established themselves as published writers of short stories, or that present colleagues managed to get university funding to attend conferences half way across the world, while she herself was not even able to get the necessary leave of absence during the semester. The problem, as always, was one of space. She was not given enough space. Her flat was too small, her study was too small, how could she be expected to write when there was not even enough space to keep her books. She had applied to the university many a time for a larger office and a larger flat, befitting her seniority in the department, but till now they had turned a deaf ear. She had even invited the very polite Mr. Ali of the Housing Department into her study at home to show him the impossibility of her cluttered desk; he had been sympathetic and assured her that as soon as one of the larger flats became available, she would be the first on the list, but for a whole year she had heard nothing. Neither was it possible to work in her office at university when one was constantly being interrupted by students wanting to discuss their own writing. Really, it was too bad.

Not that it helped, but she sometimes thought of the vast open spaces of her childhood. A childhood spent in another country, so far away from this one, half way across the globe, perched right at the edge of the world. God's own, they sometimes called it. But even in that vast open space she was constantly misplacing things, not finding them where she was certain she had left them. Even her mother, who had gone away on a train journey but never arrived where it ended. Some people said she had fallen off, some that she had jumped. Madge didn't believe either story; she was certain her mother had just been misplaced and would turn up again one day, maybe on a park bench somewhere, or on a bus. She found herself catching glimpses of the backs of women's necks or the turn of a head, or maybe even a faint perfume that made her look again. But the woman was always just out of her reach, or would disappear around a corner before Madge could get to her. She had only been twelve at the time, but she was still looking.

She had thought of returning. Her college in Christchurch would probably be only too glad to have her back. She even had a flat there though it was rented out at present, leaving her in the awkward situation of not having a place to stay when she went back in the summer holidays. Which would, of course, be winter there. But it was not that that prevented her from going back for good. It was more the lack of colour in the people that bothered her. She had lived the last fifteen years of her life surrounded by brown faces, and black faces for another seven before that, and the thought of teaching only white faces seemed strangely alien. Some of her colleagues, here and elsewhere, were white but even they came from different countries—America or Canada or South Africa. The thought of being surrounded by people who came from only one country, one culture, one colour positively frightened her. And so she had stayed on, even though the university had so far not given her the minimum space she needed to be able to write.

And now, she was convinced Uma had taken to hiding certain of her things. Her file of notes for next semester's class, for example—though what Uma could possibly want with that she could not imagine. She was aware that it was a luxury to have a

58

woman coming in twice a week to clean the flat and do the ironing, a luxury she certainly could not have afforded in her own country, but it had its own shortcomings. She had instructed Uma in no uncertain terms that she was not to move a single thing from one place to another, and Uma had in fact learned to dust around books and papers rather than even so much as lift them to dust underneath, but things still got misplaced. There had been that green and gold shawl that was the last thing her sister had given her before she had died. It had brought tears to her eyes when she discovered that it was missing, but luckily it had turned up a week later at the bottom of the laundry basket, although it was not meant to be washed. Little things like that. Yes, she would definitely have to have another little talk with Uma.

But still, one didn't give up hope. Of finding the things eventually. Maybe even of finding her mother one day. Such things did happen.

In the end Madge put on the other pair of black trousers, the ones that made her perspire behind the knees, because she didn't want to be late for her appointment. Mr. Ali of the Housing Department had called her that morning. There was a larger flat that had just become available and would she like to have a look at it?

Kaye Lee

My Life as a Line

I have become a Tube line
underground, secret,

travelling alone. Sometimes
I notice traces—a paint stripe,

trailing wires—of another line
sharing my tunnel, or we meet

momentarily by a station platform
before going our separate ways.

I am a yellow circle;
I end where I start.

I watch you, smart district green,
run parallel for three or four stops

before bending away out of sight.
Once, when I jumped my track

I rose, black as the permanent night
I'd left, to skip through Highgate Wood.

Nicola Warwick

Muntjac

At heart, I am a small deer
crossing a quiet lane.
You are always the driver
in a dark car
riding the bends.
You are pressed for time
so we meet
for the inevitable.
I always yield
to the force of steel,
rupturing the parts
I should have kept protected.
You continue,
a little winded,
metal scraping tarmac,
a crunch of gears.
I am left twitching
at the side of the road,
hoping you will catch me
in your mirror
when you look back.

Self-portrait with mourning jewellery

No-one is dead.
I wear it to follow fashion,
this lump of black gloss
at my neck.

An amulet
soft enough to cut
into the shape of an eagle
to grant me long life.

Observe the play of coal
against my pale, a sheen
like obsidian offset against
the translucence of my skin.

See how it nuzzles
the hollow where my collar bones
meet, how it waits, here,
how one stroke of force
could thrust it back
to wreck my throat.

But with this jewel
I am safe. I rub its surface
to fire the static,
attracting dust, small pieces
of debris, a carbon magnet.

Devil dark, this piece
repels malevolence,
the hexes of those skilled
in cursing, those who would
overlook me with evil eyes.

I keep it here, tight
as a choker,
nestled like an ulcer
that will not heal.

The Iceman's Wife

After seeing you off, I went back inside
to escape the early autumn chill.
I saw you melt into the morning light,
your shape fusing with the trees
at the forest edge, your arm raised
in a silent goodbye.

     The night before,
I'd watched you pack your bag,
your tools, the axe, bow and arrows
in their deerskin quiver. Then I'd
prepared food, strips of meat,
late summer fruit, thinking you'd be gone
just a week or so, one last journey
before the winter. To give you warmth
and comfort, I padded your shoes with grass.

     I remember
your last words, how we both
marvelled at the earth, the bushes
laced with spiders' webs.

Time passes slowly. Winter bites.
Perhaps you're lying broken on the rocks,
your blood spilt and frozen.
In spring, we search the white fringes
of ice, but there's no trace,
as if the earth has split and sucked you in.
I'm left trading favours for my keep.

     I'm thinking of taking
another husband. I'm missing
your smell, your ways, the heat of you
beside me, your skin newly raw
from the tattoo needle.

I will weep like a good wife should,
then take a man who won't stray,
who'll stay by the fire and leave
travelling to the fools, a man who'll soothe
the nightmares of you coming back as
I'm suckling another man's child.

By summer, you're just a memory,
a tale for the bard, slipping from me
melting like water from ice.

Everest

This is a land of nothing but rock
and snow, low clouds that coat the air,
conceal the sky.

Altitude sucks at lungs.
Eyes safe behind dark glasses,
lips crack, fingers spilt.

We're on a quest for a corpse,
glimpsed, a mirage in the snow.

On the north face, a patch
of white that is not snow;
the wind-whipped flesh of a back
exposed for punishment.

Cold has preserved skin,
worn it to the sheen of plastic,
a mannequin dumped as a prank.

We pause and shiver.
He's face down, a child
playing hide-and–seek,
still waiting for the call.

Our slow hands swarm the body,
parting thin layers of cotton, linen,
stilled at his name:
George Mallory.

We want to finish his story,
grant him the right to burial,
a tomb of stones—
but did he reach the summit?

Our hands fumble, turn over
a ragged sock, an unpaid bill,
peel back decades
of not knowing.

Feeding the Cat
Lindsay Stanberry-Flynn

Julian looked at his watch: Hermione would be waiting.

'What will you do when you get back?' George asked.

Julian stared out of the bus window.

'I said—'

'I heard what you said.' Julian kept his eyes fixed on a woman in a tweed coat, waiting at the traffic lights. Mother had a coat just like that.

'So what's with the silent treatment? You get more like *her* all the time.'

The lights changed and the tweed coat set off across the road. Julian's gaze followed it until the tweed faded into the crowd.

George jabbed his elbow into Julian's side. 'I want to know what you're going to do when you get back.'

The bus jerked forward. 'I'm going to feed Hermione.'

'Damn that moggy. Come for a pint.'

'No.'

'Then I'll come to the house.' George raised his voice. 'We can start clearing stuff out.'

'Callous sod! She's only been dead for a week.'

A man in the front seat of the bus turned round and stared. Perhaps they should have had the hire car from the crematorium, but Mother had stipulated it wasn't necessary. Nobody saw what you did afterwards.

'There's bound to be something worth a bit,' George said.

'Nothing you'll get your hands on.'

'How come?'

'She hated you.'

Julian stood in the kitchen, a tin of cat food in one hand, the opener in the other, while Hermione wove her way backwards and forwards between his legs, her body insinuating itself round first the left and then the right. He closed his eyes. The continuous movement was like a mother's palm stroking the forehead of a sick child. He felt himself swaying. His fingers tightened round the tin.

'Christ!' Needles of pain pricked his shin. His eyes shot open and he looked down: Hermione had attached her claws to his leg through the material of his trousers. He bit his lip and let her hang there. He glanced at the serrated edge of the open tin. It wouldn't be difficult to drag it across his wrist. He would watch the wound open up, the blood spurt out. Would clench his teeth against the pain. It would be hot, intense, would block out the hole in the pit of his stomach.

He kicked Hermione from his leg and grabbed a fork to push the meat concoction into the bowl. The stench made him gag. Hermione's purr echoed round the kitchen units. He dropped the tin and fork into the sink and picked up a pen.

Sheets of paper were blu-tacked to the wall above the worktop. The words JULIAN/MOOD headed one sheet; and JULIAN/CHORES another. Julian's gaze skimmed a third sheet: HERMIONE/FOOD/APPETITE. The columns were filled-in in Mother's stilted writing: 'salmon morsels/dainty; tuna chunks/reluctant; plaice titbits/choosy.' His hand moved across the page: Thursday 10th, evening feed. He looked down at Hermione. She'd moved bits of meat from the bowl on to the kitchen floor—the floor he'd scrubbed that morning—and was growling over them, her paw pulling them closer, her back arched. Julian's eyes returned to the list. Slashing the pen across the page, he inserted 'cow's brains' and 'voracious'.

He scrutinised the sheets of paper until he found FUNERALS. He ripped the page from the wall. Blu-tack was still attached, and it came away with a sliver of paint, leaving a patch of bare plaster in the recently applied magnolia. The patch was heart-shaped.

Julian glimpsed a shadow passing in front of the window, followed by a dark outline at the back door. He started to retreat, shuffling his slippered feet into the hall, where he hid behind the door into the kitchen and peered through the gap.

'Julian!' a voice called. It was a soft, female voice. 'Julian, it's Mary.'

Julian felt the muscles of his face contract. He put his fingers to his lips—the corners were raised, as if he was smiling. Mary lived in a house in the next street with her two children. She didn't have a husband, and Julian didn't know why. But he knew Mary was small and pretty, with eyes the colour of bluebells, and she always waved at him from her window when he passed by with the shopping. She was in the front garden once and he'd stopped to admire the roses. He must have been braver then. 'They smell gorgeous,' she said, and he bent down to sniff. The fragrance was heavy and sweet, and he pushed his face closer to the rose. When he stood up, she laughed. 'Come here,' she said, and brushed his cheek. 'You've got pollen all over you.' Her touch had tickled his skin.

'Julian!' she called again now.

He heard the scrape of the back door on the kitchen tiles. Through his peephole, he could see half of Mary standing in the middle of the room.

'I was sorry to hear about your mum,' she said, as if he was next to her and not skulking behind the door.

He took a couple of steps towards the kitchen. She was holding a dish with a glass lid. 'I've made a casserole for tea,' she said. 'I thought I'd bring some round. I don't expect you feel like cooking.'

'Thank you,' Julian heard himself saying. 'You're very kind.'

Mary put the dish on the table. 'You're very kind, Julian. Your mum was lucky to have you. We all thought so.' Her hand touched his arm.

Under his cotton shirt, Julian's skin burned.

Mary turned to the oven and pulled open the door. She slid the dish on to the middle shelf and flicked the switch. The light shone from inside the oven. 'It's on a low heat, so you can have it when you're ready.'

Julian smiled again, but his face ached from the unaccustomed movement.

'Bye, Julian,' he heard Mary call from the back door.

In the living room, Julian sat in Mother's big armchair. It felt strange—he'd never dared sit there before. He picked up his pen and rested the paper on a book: FUNERALS.

Mother had liked funerals; on a good week, she'd go to two, and she was meticulous afterwards; awarding marks out of ten for every aspect. The woman who lived at number forty-six had only managed an overall three: 'such a shame', Mother had said, 'no style, no taste.' Nothing less than an eight or nine would do for hers.

Julian's pen was poised over the sheet of paper. The first column was headed EULOGY. Now this column should have been an outright 10. He remembered the day they got back from the hospital with the diagnosis. She'd sat at the kitchen table writing, crossing out, rewriting for so long that she missed *Coronation Street*. He said to her '*Corrie's* on, Mother. Do you want your cup of tea while you watch it?' But she waved him away.

'It will be a good one,' he'd told the vicar when he handed the sealed envelope over a couple of days ago. 'She wrote it herself.' The vicar raised his eyebrows: 'Not leaving anything to chance then?' He winked and smiled, but Julian couldn't see how either was appropriate in the circumstances. He should have known then the eulogy would be a travesty of what Mother had written. There was no mention of his long nights by her bed when the pain was bad, the clearing away the bowl of vomit, the pot of piss, the painstaking attention to her demands. No. 'Her son, Julian, always tried hard to do his best,' he heard the vicar say. Tried hard to do his best! It was like a poxy school report, when the teacher couldn't bring himself to say—this boy is stupid. He held the pen over the eulogy column and wrote 5.

He moved on to the next column: LINE-UP. Mother used to deduct three marks straight away if there were fewer than six principal mourners, so he'd tried to get a good turnout. He was first in line, him being the eldest son by fifteen minutes, and then George. He was sure Mother would have forbidden George from coming to the funeral if she could. It was the vicar who insisted on telling him when it was—Julian would never have let him know. He'd watched a programme once about a man who'd been ill on and off all his life. They thought they'd found a tumour in his stomach, but when they opened him up, they discovered this ball made from hair, bits of teeth and bones. Apparently, he'd been a twin and the other baby had died in the womb and he'd swallowed it. Julian felt sick at the thought that it could have happened to him with George. It was bad enough putting up with him alive, but if he'd had to carry a decomposing lump around inside him...

Next in the line-up was Aunt Florrie. Julian hadn't wanted her at the funeral, but when Mrs Hardcastle from next door said she had a hospital appointment, and Mother's cousin thought she had flu, Julian had no choice but to let Florrie come and hope her twitch had got better.

He couldn't bring himself to write the 4 that he knew, in his heart of hearts, the line-up deserved, so he slid the pen over to the next column: GRIEF. He'd tried to be stoical, like Mother said you should. For her, not a tear shed had been a definite 10. It was Florrie who'd had a white lace handkerchief pressed to her nose during the ceremony, and as for George…

Why had George been bawling his eyes out? It wasn't as if Mother had ever had a good word to say for him. Not since he dropped his gay bombshell anyway. That's what she always called it—the night of the gay bombshell. She used to mouth the words in case the neighbours heard. Her lips would be contorted, which made her false teeth slip out, and she had to click them back into place.

Julian inserted 5 under GRIEF. Now for the next column. He hadn't expected such a tussle over the music.

'It's not a suitable hymn,' the vicar had argued.

'It's what she wanted.'

'Spears, bows, swords—it's too war-like. Bereavement should be a time of love—reconciliation.'

'It's what she wanted,' Julian insisted.

And he'd won, although, as he stood in the front row, gaze fixed on the mahogany coffin, poised for the lid to rise at any moment—she wouldn't give in as easily as that, would she? —the words of the hymn felt like cloth in his mouth. 'I will not cease from mental fight.' He couldn't fight; he was so tired he felt his bones might crumple and only his new black suit would remain standing in the pew. Something touched his hand and he looked down. George's fingers had closed round his bunched fist. George's hand was warm and smooth, and for a moment Julian was in the playground on their first day at school. They were scared, he remembered, and they'd held hands.

Julian scribbled 6 in the music column and moved on: FLOWERS. He was about to write 10—Mother had chosen the chrysanthemums herself—when the doorbell rang. Hardly anyone rang the bell, but last week there'd been a succession of visitors, the doctor, the undertakers, the vicar—a whole procession of deathmongers—and the sound sliced through Julian. He wouldn't answer, he decided. Then it rang again. And again.

He edged to the door and peered round it. The flap on the letterbox banged open.

'I know you're in there, Julian. Open the door.' George's voice pierced the gloomy hall.

Julian withdrew his head.

'No point hiding. I saw your shape through the glass.'

George's voice drilled into his brain: 'Come on, mate. Don't stay in there on your own.'

'Go away.'

'I need the company even if you don't.'

Mother would have had a fit at George hollering out there; half the neighbourhood would be glued to their windows.

Julian stuck his head into the hallway again. 'Get lost, George!' He could see the glint of eyes through the letterbox. 'She'd go mad if she was here.'

'I don't give a stuff about her. Nor should you—you can have a life at last.'

'I've got a life.'

'I mean a proper one.' George's voice grew louder. 'Without *her*.'

Pain spiked the back of Julian's eyes. He clenched his fists, the nails digging into the palms. *Don't cry. Whatever you do, don't cry.* He took a couple of steps towards the front door. He'd slam the letterbox shut on George's fingertips.

'That's it, mate,' George called. 'Open the door.'

'Go away!' Julian's chest felt as if it would burst.

'I bet she's told you how long you must grieve. But it's up to you now. You can tear up her stupid bits of paper.'

'I've got to fill them in.'

''Course you haven't. It's not as if she ever cared about *you*.'

Julian fell back against the wall. He slipped down it, until he was crouching near the floor.

George gave up at last and went away. But not before one last bellow through the letterbox: 'I'll be back tomorrow, and the day after. You'll have to open up eventually.'

Julian sat on the floor in the darkening hall. Silence breathed around him. 'She loved me,' he whispered. 'I know she did.' Just because she'd never said it, didn't mean she didn't feel it. He hauled himself to his feet and slowly climbed the stairs.

He fastened his hand round the doorknob of Mother's room. He hadn't been in there since the day she died. After the undertakers had removed the body—they'd struggled getting her eighteen-stone frame round the corner at the top of the stairs—he'd gone in and stripped the bed. He took out new Egyptian cotton sheets she'd been saving for best, and remade it. He removed the bottles of medicine, the potty, and all the detritus of

71

her illness, and scrubbed every surface. He sprinkled rosewater onto the pillows and the curtains, like she used to.

Now he pushed open the door, blinking at the scent of the rosewater, the green swirls on the smoothed-down duvet cover, the beige fleece slippers beside the bed, as if she'd just stepped out of them, the pink towelling dressing gown on the back of the door. His gaze swivelled to the window, expecting almost to see her standing there, net curtain twitching between her fingers: *That Maud Johnson's put her bin out early again.*

He crossed to the bed and sat down. On top of a small chest of drawers next to it were her glasses, magazines, the tumbler for her teeth. There used to be a photograph in a brass frame of a young woman and a man in a soldier's uniform. One day George had said: 'Is that man my dad?' and her hand had struck the back of his head. Then the photo disappeared.

Julian edged open the top drawer of the chest. He felt a draught at his back and glanced over his shoulder, afraid to find her standing there. Watching. There was no one. He turned back —the drawer was empty. He pulled open the second one—empty. The third—empty. He knew the drawers used to contain letters, cards, photos—he'd seen her look for things. When had she cleared them all out? In that last week? He rushed to the chest on the other side of the bed. Top drawer—empty. Second drawer—empty. Third—wait. There was a box.

He lifted the lid. He picked up a ball of tissue paper and opened it out. Inside was a tooth, a child's baby tooth. Underneath was a curl of hair, blond and fluffy. It must have been George's; Julian's hair had always been darker than his brother's. At the bottom of the box Julian found a small rectangular photo: a toddler's face, mouth pulled back in a grin. Julian turned the photo over: *G 2 yrs 3 mnths.*

He flung the box at the wall. He didn't need to look any further, pull clothes from drawers, search the top of the wardrobe: he knew there would be no box for him. He stumbled to his feet. The smell of the rosewater clung to his skin, cloying his nose, his mouth, reaching down into his throat.

He crossed the room and slammed the door shut behind him. He put his elbows on the banister and leaned against it, forcing air into his lungs. George was right: she hadn't loved him; probably never did. The white-hot spear that had pierced his brain when he saw the photo cooled. His breathing grew easier and steadied.

Julian knew what he would do. He would go downstairs. He would take scissors from the drawer in the kitchen and he would cut all her lists into tiny pieces. At the window, Hermione's mouth would open in a silent yowl, but he would stare her out. He would set the table; he might even look for a candle; and he would lift Mary's casserole from the oven and eat it. He'd wash the dish and tomorrow, or the next day he might take it back to Mary. One day he'd phone George. Or would he?

John Mackay

The astronaut's wife

When he goes on a trip, I lock the doors,
slip into my leisure suit and somersault
across the sitting room. I eat takeaways,
let silvery dust settle on the surfaces.

I imagine him up there, tied
by an umbilical cord to his landing craft.
He is pawing rocks with sausage fingers,
leaving his mark in ton-weight boots.

When he first showed me the night sky,
I wanted to pluck the aloof moon
and warm it in my hands. Later, he filled
my ear with names of the seas: Cleverness,

Fecundity, Serenity. I mouthed the Latin—
Mare Cognitum, the Sea That Has Become Known.
He took me round the world, explained
the enigma of ancient craters.

Now, I climb jagged mountains alone. The air
is thin when I reach the summit. If I leap
off the top into nothingness, will my body
become weightless? I want to find out.

The return

A month ago, you carried me
on your shoulders across these stones
and into the lap of salt water. You said
not to worry about clouds because
you had the sun in your pocket.

Now, I have the pock-faced moon
for company. It looks down on me
and frowns at my blistered feet.
Wind rushes from behind a bluff
and lifts me clean into the air.

There's the spot where you brushed
sand from your trousers, picked up
your briefcase and told me you had to go.
You pressed the sun into my palm
and said it would guard me in the dark.

I waved as you slowly disappeared
under the surface, and wondered
if you would make it back
in time. The last thing I saw
was your bald head like an island.

If you were here for my birthday,
you could watch me flying
all on my own—clear of the stones,
into the all-embracing night,
a copper coin clenched in my hand.

The gathering

Yes, it is dead, heavy as a man's heart,
but it is loved. Pinned by six prongs

to a stainless platter, it reflects
the sheen of our admiration, carried

like a baby down carpeted aisle
to the altar. A communal *Oooh* exudes

and somebody yelps. It quivers,
there is a great uprush of steam, the last

of its breath disappearing into Artex.
Breast, leg, rump, all denuded.

We fear the moment when it is gone
and we must regard each other

rather than this dismantled cathedral,
the high dome of the bones.

We pick what remains from walls
and ceiling, and see inside its ruined home.

Annie Bien

Ripples

Night clings to the upper lip,
too early in the season to count
cricket chirps.

The throb of news slips from my eyes
into the electric fan, whirring away
the images of fish stranded

on the beach, a spread of finned pebbles.
An egret shivers. My cat turns, his toes
twitch to a dream of the apartment world

where natural disasters occur
as the wind blowing rain
through the window,

knocking orchid petals
into the water bowl.
I lift the screen
to release a ladybug.

300 birds, eleven men, and porn

Smeared sand, beached corpses,
angel wings coated in grime
necks twist as mouths gag.

Chatter on the wind:
the men you hire on the rigs
are worth the price of three little pigs.

Blow, blow, the pyre comes down
burning bodies
engulfed in blazing waters.

So far from the sea,
landlocked brains
tainted by boredom
seek arousal
by switching screens.

The pregnant dolphin's
instincts to protect her young
is rendered helpless
by an escape key.

Precautions
Natalie Donbavand

I'm in love. I touch the dark down of hair; it feels damp and smells vaguely metallic. Puckered lips mouth in sleep. Her fists furl and unfurl, grabbing handfuls of air, a substance still alien to her. If I hold my fingers in the right place, she will grasp them, her petal nails deceptively sharp. For someone so small she has surprising strength.

The feel of her flesh against mine is electric. We have a connection her and me. It is a flow of energy, something from the beginning of time. The talcum sweetness of her hands fills me with longing. I want to pick her up and squeeze until her flesh morphs back into mine.

She has come from me, but she is not like me. She is not like her father. She looks vital. Blue eyes against black lashes; their clarity is frightening. Her features are shoots; an idea is growing inside me.

When I try to think back, it feels like untangling dreadlocks. Only the first bit is clear. My first boyfriend; he had dreadlocks. I was seventeen and in my second year at sixth form. Geoff was in his first year at Uni. I would spend my Sunday afternoons in a rank bedsit in the centre of Manchester. The damp masked with incense and the cracks with posters of Ganesh. While I did my A levels, Geoff sat at home praying for world peace, honing his magical powers and practising past life regression. He wasn't the boyfriend I had expected, but I was a late starter—he seemed to love me. The trouble with Geoff was sex. My Dad had been clear about sex; if I got pregnant he would be furious, if I had an abortion, he would never talk to me again; the Catholic rock and a hard place. Geoff wanted sex.

Lying in a BO saturated duvet on a drizzling Sunday, I prepared my self for my first time. I bargained with the higher powers; *Dear God, if you make sure I don't get pregnant, I'll promise never to have sex with anyone other than Geoff.* Then I began fondling Geoff's penis. He got an erection. Using my initiative, I fumbled a condom over the top of it. Geoff grabbed my hand.

'Don't get me wrong babe, I'm glad you want to do it, It's just I don't enjoy sex with condoms, it doesn't twist my melon man'

He was always quoting The Happy Mondays at me.

'Hum hmm.'

'Yeah, it's just that I get turned on by—like—y'know.'

'No. What?'

'By the wetness of your flower.'

I paused to consider. A mental picture of my dad was quickly eclipsed by an image of God. It wasn't the benevolent God who visited me in church. This one was a burning ball of righteousness. I could not get pregnant.

'Hum hmm. Well—maybe I'll look into the pill.'

I checked in on the image of God in my head, there was the deepening of a frown, but it was not a 'No Way!'

'Oh. No way!'

I jumped.

'What?'

'I'm not havin' all those hormones gettin' into me.'

'I'll be the one taking them.'

'Look, that's your choice. I don't want any chemical hormone crap gettin' into me. I might grow bozoomas.'

'And how exactly would it get into you?'

'Through osmosis babe.' Geoff was doing a degree in environmental science.

'Osmosis through your penis?'

'Yeah, exactly right.'

'Hmmm. I'm not particularly happy about using the withdrawal method.'

'Me neither babe, I want to like—fill you with my love potion.'

'So what do you suggest?'

'Magic.'

The ball of righteousness bounced ferociously. Heresy was one step too far.

'Magic?'

'Yeah, honestly, watch this.'

He lay on his back, draped a lazy arm over my breasts and started to masturbate.

One minute later we sat examining the semen freckling his pubic hair and stomach.

'See?' he said beaming down at it.

'What?'

'I'm infertile.'

'How——?'

'Well, look at it.'

'Yes?'

'Come on babe, I've been manifesting this for weeks.'

'No really, I don't know.'

'Ok. Fertile semen would be white, my semen is clear, which means that I am infertile.'

'I'm not sure I'd call that clear.' I leaned closer, my nose inadvertently catching a stray droplet.

'Babe, it's definitely clear.'

'Hmmm'

I wasn't uninformed. I knew that you couldn't get pregnant from the swimming pool, or a toilet seat, or oral sex. However I had been raised on miracles. There was no such thing as completely impossible.

In the clinic, Doctor Llewellyn Jones stared; a warm blush crept up my neck. I focussed on the stainless steel of his stethoscope.

'So let me just check. You haven't actually had sex?'

'Not exactly.' I squirmed.

'Did his penis enter your vagina without a condom?'

'No.'

'So he didn't ejaculate inside your vagina?'

'Not inside. No.'

'Did he ejaculate near your vagina?'

Of course, near was all relative. It was in the same room as my vagina.

'Yes.'

'How near?'

I would have to embellish the truth a little to get what I wanted.

'About a centimetre.'

'Well now, it is very unlikely that sperm will jump a centimetre through mid air to reach your vagina'

He chuckled.

I stared down at the thinning carpet around my chair. Doctor Jones' feet were extremely small. *Please God may he give it me. Please God may he give it me.* I must have chanted aloud because his expression suddenly changed.

'However, as you are clearly very anxious about it, I will give you emergency contraception this once, but you should book an appointment to discuss other, long term methods of contraception.'

I nodded and tried hard to form boundaries between external and internal dialogue.

As I was leaving, prescription in hand, I turned—he was looking at me, a funny, sort of sad look.

'Is there anyone at home you can talk to about this—your mum—maybe an aunty?'

'My mum isn't around.'

I didn't wait for a response.

I never did experience long term. Geoff chucked me a fortnight later for a girl who was less 'uptight' than me. I was more upset than I knew what to do with. I tried praying, but God seemed pleased by the news. Even my earthly father seemed unable to offer any comfort.

'Never mind Kiddo, you've always got your old man.'

I am weak. It is official. I have to spend a few nights in hospital for observation. All around me women are packing up their tiny bundles. I must stay. I lost a lot of blood during the birth. I had to have a transfusion. This alien blood, it doesn't feel like mine. It seems to be causing chaos inside.

The nurse comes in to clean my stitches. They are tender to the touch, but the pain is a kiss in comparison to the birth.

'Healing nicely. A few salty baths back home and you won't even notice.'

'Hmmm.'

She looks over at the baby.

'Isn't the body an amazing thing?'

'That's exactly what the midwife said.'

She laughs.

'I'd never really thought about it that way before. The midwife said something else—'

'What love?'

She is writing something in marker pen on my chart.

'The midwife—I wasn't pushing or breathing or something that I was supposed to do and she said; don't fight, tune into it, it's your body and it's working for you.'

'What?' She looks distracted now. She has other people to see.

'I've just never thought of it that way before—my body—mine and working for me.'

She shakes her head and goes to leave. . .

'Nurse—have you ever felt like you're not yourself? Like you spend more time doing stuff for other people than for yourself?'

She snorts, 'It's part of the joy of being a woman love. Try not to think about it too much now, get some rest. When's dad arriving?'

'Half an hour'

'Good. Time for you to have a little rest.'

I nod. She smiles, draws the curtains around me and bustles away. I hear her shout instructions to a colleague at the other end of the ward. I try to settle back on the pillows, but my mind feels skittish and my thoughts come in flashes as though I have never known anything before. 'It is part of the joy of being a woman,' and to that sort of woman it is. She is capable. Her children will be capable. She will do lots of things for lots of people, but she will do them because she wants to do them. She is womanly. What do I want?

I look at the tiny woman beside me and I can't breathe.

Damien. We were in our second year at Manchester University. It was a meeting of minds. He wanted me to go on the pill, so that we could experience a 'physical closeness, to rival our mental intimacy,' one in three women in Britain were on it. A ninety eight percent success rate didn't seem too bad. I clarified the statistics by counting out one hundred matches on the kitchen table and colouring two black. Strangely, that didn't seem so comforting. Also there was a choice. Properly researched, I realized that there are twenty three brands of combined oral contraceptive pill, all claiming to be the most effective. I asked Dr Llewellyn Jones.

'Oh, one's much the same as another.'

Could I trust a fifty five year old welsh midget with my body? In the end I had to go for the name. It was the only way of doing it. Yasmin sounded too ditzy to be relied upon; Minulet—too much like an 18th century dance; Ovysmen a combination of ovum and semen that seemed to court disaster; Cyclessa sounded like the name of a seer, thus the future and ultimately pregnancy because 'babies are the future'. Eventually I chose Brevinor, mainly because it sounded like the name of an Anglo Saxon warrior queen. If anything would be able to stop those tenacious tadpoles it would be her. In retrospect I realised that my pill choice could be blamed on my study of *Beowulf*.

Like the pill—Damien promised a lot. Damien was everything that Geoff wasn't. He was an over achiever; captain of the rowing team, an active member of the NUS and to top it all off, he was heading for a first in Computer Science. He was socially competent and came from a large and welcoming family. What were the chances of him staying with me? I didn't trust Damien. I didn't trust the pill. I concentrated on not getting pregnant. I developed insomnia.

It was midnight. Damien's broad frame was looming over me and taking up much of my boxy, halls of residence room. He was wearing a rugby shirt and nothing else.

'I just don't understand why this is so hard. We spend more time not having sex than actually having it.'

'Forty-four, forty-five—Ssh, I 'm counting.'

My pill packets lay empty in front of me. Pills scattered the shag pile.

'You've been checking for hours.'

'I need to be sure.'

'Look, you've not missed one. You just took Wednesday's pill from Tuesday's place in the packet look.'

'Get off!'

'Can't we just use condoms tonight?'

'It isn't safe enough. I can't get pregnant.'

'I love you. I just want to be intimate with you. You're letting your issues with your mother ruin us.'

I ignore him.

'Not everyone you love is going to leave you.'

'You are.'

'You're pushing me away.'

I felt a million words bubbled to the surface, but none of them made their way to my lips. His GCSE psychology annoyed me.

He left without his trousers. The doorframe shuddered. I continued poking at the fibres of carpet, laughter bubbling up inside me—I was searching the shag while Damien was searching for one.

University nights were long and often torturous. I used to absorb those dark hours with parties; drink would lull me to sleep for a few hours, only to wake me up with a sore head and a jumbled mind. Sometimes I would wander the campus talking to the all-night porters, visiting each building in turn, before returning to the start to retrace my steps.

After the argument with Damien, I wandered into the Student's Union and sat in the ladies' toilet, my head resting on the rim of the toilet bowel. I cried a lot. I vomited. I started to read the right-on-philosophy-student Nietzsche graffiti dotted around the cubical, but following it hurt my overtired brain. Just when I was beginning to truly despair, the waters of the toilet bowl began to swirl and the bearded face of God appeared. He pointed at the cubical wall. I searched, following his line of vision. It was there, plastered over the middle class scrawl—a little blue smiling telephone; something friendly and honest amid all of the biro bullshit:

NIGHTLINE
Student help line and drop-in,
For information and support.
Call us on 01257 667788
Or drop in at Harborough College

The beaded curtain savaged me on entrance. Sounds of my struggle ushered in the presence of a lanky male.

'Would you like to come in?'

'I'm trying.'

'Oh, yes, of course sorry.'

He hovered around me, picking ineffectually at strings of beads. He was clearly terrified to touch me just in case I was a victim of abuse.

'That's it!' I pulled a final bead from my hand bag.

'Ok. Do you want to come through? We have comfy chairs.'

'Ok.'

The skinny boy took a seat opposite.

We sat facing each other for some minutes. He sat very still with his hands clasped neatly in his lap. There was soothing music playing in the background and wisps of incense smoke curled up to the ceiling. My fidgeting, hiccupping and sobbing seemed to be ruining the mellow atmosphere. The boy looked disgruntled. Clearly I wasn't being soothed quickly enough.

'Would you like a tissue?'

I took one.

'I'm here to listen, if you want to talk.'

That old chestnut.

'Well, you know, it's just that—um—I think something is

wrong with me.'

'You think something is wrong with you?'

'Yes.'

It all seemed to gush out.

'I'm really paranoid about getting pregnant. I never want to have sex. I lose all my boyfriends because they say I'm too uptight. I have an unhealthily close relationship with my father. I never sleep. I go to church every Sunday, even though I don't want to. I have no idea what I want to do with my life. I keep thinking about trying to find my mum, but I'm scared. I can't concentrate on my degree and worst of all I keep having visions.' 'You keep having visions?'

Clearly active listening training had not prepared him for this. He kept glancing at the panic button in the left hand corner of the room.

'Yeah, sometimes I see God.'

Now he was the one doing the hiccuping.

'And how does that make you feel?'

I burst out crying. The boy suggested I see a doctor. I thought of Doctor Llewellyn Jones and cried harder.

Whilst I was being counselled, Damien had undertaken a course of sex therapy with the blonde social secretary of the Junior Common Room Committee—a political move. I struggled for a while and then moved back home.

I lean over and take the bundle from the cot beside me. I have half an hour in which she is truly mine. I doubt we will ever get this time again. I am her mother, they have not held her yet—for her they do not exist. It feels like making the first footprints in the snow. Soon her father and her grandfather will come and her life will be mixed up with theirs forever—turned from white to grey. For now she is mine. Is this how my mother felt when she held me? For all these years, I presumed she left because she didn't want me. Perhaps she left to keep this time perfect—she did not want to share me. I will not leave my daughter.

I had spent years trying not to get pregnant to keep the men in my life and now Tristan wanted the opposite. Doctor Jones' white head was just visible, poking up from between my thighs. The stirrups were hurting my ankles and forceps created a chill that reached my core. I felt a tug. Doctor Jones straightened up, smiling and waving a tiny plastic 'T'—my coil.

'Got it. That didn't hurt now did it?'

'Not compared to the going in.'

'Ah. Now wait till you experience labour.'

I rolled my eyes and pulled up my knickers. It felt like a loss. The coil might have been excruciatingly painful to have fitted, but it had been 98% effective and I hadn't needed to remember anything.

'It'll be a few months before your cycle settles down again, but then there should be no detrimental effects.'

'My fertility won't be reduced?'

'How old are you?'

'Twenty two.'

'Young thing like you should be pregnant in no time.'

'Oh Good. Hmmm, my partner is older—forty, that won't make any difference will it?'

He raised his eyebrows.

'Men can father children into their eighties. All part of nature's great plan.'

He seemed to drift off into some kind of reverie.

'Now then, It's best to wait two years between children, so if you want to come back and have it fitted after you've given birth, I can assure you, the pain will be considerably less.'

'Thanks.'

I swung my self down off the examination table. Doctor Jones sat in his chair swinging his legs, they didn't touch the floor.

'I told you the story about the patient who got pregnant whilst using the coil—the baby came out with the coil held in its fist. Laughing it was.'

It wasn't my idea to try for a baby. It was one of Tristan's dinner party brain waves. I hated going to dinner parties. I hated going to them with Tristan because we were such a stereotype. He was the managing director of the paper company where my dad worked, I was his PA. Before I had been promoted to the lofty position of Tristan's PA, I had been my father's PA. Tristan's dinner party friends were managing directors with wives who were managing directors. There was so much to hide.

The baby idea came from a fairly typical evening. We were at the home of Felix, who was a partner in the law firm that represented Papertrax. Felix lived in a huge detached house in

87

Alderly Edge, an affluent suburb of Manchester. I was concentrating on remembering every detail of the decoration, because my dad loved details about the 'well-to-do'. There wasn't much to remember, it was all minimalist cream and gold. It was an intimate gathering, Felix and Hermione, Sancha and Russel and Tristan and I. We sipped vodka tonics and reclined on cream leather arm chairs, watching gas flames leap from tastefully placed rocks there was 'nothing as common as a fireplace.' Tristan and Felix talked; not to each other, just over each other. The two other women, both in their forties eyed me suspiciously. They were both tall and blonde, the kind of women who had ponies when they were girls. One of them was pregnant and sat caressing her baby bump. I felt short and dark and ordinary. The women exchanged significant looks; I knew the questions were coming.

'So, where did you two meet?'

It was the worst of all the questions because it demanded a lie. I couldn't tell the truth—'Oh yes Hermione/Sancha, it's a lovely story; I was at a work's party. I was really drunk and tried to commit suicide in the stationary cupboard; luckily Tristan found me unconscious with sick in my hair and took me to casualty.' Instead I said what they wanted to hear.

'I was taking minutes for my dad at a meeting and Tristan was there and we got talking over coffee afterwards.'

'I see.'

'Of course, we haven't seen Tris in ages, not since the divorce. Did you ever meet his wife? Hideous woman. What was her name?'

'Belinda.'

'Yes. She was infertile, never told Tris, even though he had always made it clear that children were part of the game plan. They tried for two years, then there were tests, turns out she'd known all along.'

'That must have been really hard for her.'

They exchanged looks. It wasn't the response they wanted.

'How old are you, if you don't mind me asking?'

'Twenty-five.'

'Gosh—so young. I was still at university then—PHD.'

I thought about telling them that I had done two years at university. I could have finished. I was bright enough; I just had some 'personal issues.'

'Mind you,' Hermione/Sancha continued 'I'm glad I've had the experience of a successful career. Now I'm really ready to enjoy this baby. It's perfectly safe to have children after forty now. Emotionally it's better—more to give.'

'Of course darling! Forty is the new thirty.'

That's when it dawned on me; they thought Tristan was using me—I was a baby making machine, a last ditch attempt at the family he wanted.

Tristan's eyes follow Hermione's bump all evening. Somewhere around the cheese and biscuits, God appeared by Hermione's side. He pointed at the bump and gave me the thumbs up. I imagined telling my father I was pregnant and the scary thing was, I knew he would be pleased.

My finger is held in her fist. This morning she didn't exist—not as herself. I feel as though I don't have a self. I remember what my dad said when he drove me to hospital, 'I hope this baby is just like you. I'm so proud of you.' What did I do to make him proud? I went to church. I did as I was told. I married Tristan. All the other things I put him through—all of the difficult bits, the bits that were me—they aren't mentioned; I am making him a granddad. A year ago, I would have been delighted to have pleased him, now I find that making him happy does not guarantee my own happiness.

I look at the little life in my arms, and I know that I don't want her to be like me—unsure of everything. My watch tells me that I have fifteen minutes before dad and Tristan arrive and it all begins again. They will overpower me. I do not know how to teach her to be different. I hold her to my breast. She gives me courage.

I place her back in the cot. Even this momentary separation induces panic, as though my strength will leave with the warmth of her body. I pull the curtains round the bed. There are no cracks. My hold-all is stowed in the bedside cupboard. I release it slowly, making as little noise as possible. I pull on jeans, breathing deeply through the pain. My nightdress and dressing gown are stuffed tightly into the bottom of the bag—the perfect mattress. I lay my baby on top and place a finger to her lips. A bundled-up towel replaces her in the crib. The zip closing hides her from view and I feel myself falter. I act before I can think—the curtain is pulled back. I walk down the ward, past all the husbands, fathers, brothers, mothers and sisters, with all the confidence I can muster. There will be a way to work it out.

Barbara Cumbers

Portrait of a marriage

A boat is rising in the garden
like a whale coming up to breathe.
The lawn's surface breaks
on its roundness, a rose bush

is pushed aside, a cherry tree,
a bed of irises. The man
bends wood to the boat's command,
he chisels, he planes. He is silent.

The woman sees her garden
diminish. She hangs the washing
in new places, tends fewer smaller plants.
Always she looks towards the house,

teaching her children a strange religion
whose god is of desert and dryness.
She knows no meaning
for transom, gunwale, bulkhead,

and the ways of wood and water
are not hers. The couple
are bound beyond language,
their conversation unimaginable.

The morning after

...is calm, though wind ripped through the night.
We emerge from the tent our house became,
shellshocked, our horizons altered.

The cypresses that remain
stand to attention,
soldiers at the funeral of a comrade,
showing no emotion.
Less wellbred, the shed
has shifted slightly, crooked
like the face of a child
that's trying not to cry.

Elsewhere the garden strives to look
as if nothing has happened—
roots burrow into earth
and the house has solid foundations again.

A light breeze combs the fallen cypress
softly, as if apologising,
as a small boy might to broken toys.

Phil Madden

Shore Love

Eventually, I come too close.

They rise slowly, pre panic.

Self controlled confetti.

Re land on reach

of safer sight.

The balance of distance restored.

Red, computer, toothbrush

Some days I think of days.
Some days yawn, get up,
live, yawn again, curl up,
in a perfect arc of function.

When I looked at the photographs,
there were times that were times,
there were times that were good.

Some days that end,
I do not see begin.

Some stop being days,
splinter to joy.
Some become blood,
 clotted and spilt.

Some days are not days.
Many are trains.
Some days can be anything.
Red, say, computer, toothbrush.

Some days Humpty Dumpty
is in Afghanistan,
his guts spilling out,
his mates stuffing them back,
until the medic arrives.

Some days there is only
blind faith in the queue.

Moments, meanwhile,
just sail on serene,
as my thoughts search for days.

Apples to Auschwitz

Around: terror, shit.
Outside, despite,
seeing the moon through a crack in the truck.
Thinking of apple slices.

Martin Willitts Jr

Landscape with a Church at Twilight

Based on the painting, *"Landscape with a Church at Twilight,"*
Van Gogh, 1883

Listen to the wrestling angels
during the period between forgiveness and madness.
See the church in the vacant fields.
There is nothing here for me in the absolution
or emptiness in outstretched hands of the land.
I can beg all I want to. Ring bells for salvation
until my hands are rope burns. No one will listen.
There is only emptiness.

I prostrate myself on canvases of immense loss.
The voices tell me what I need.
I am abandoned in terrifying blue so grey,
it is the color of angel wings when ashamed.
This is the hour between tomorrow and yesterday.
I do not belong in either place.
The roof of the world is collapsing on my head.
The sun is below the horizon refusing to arrive.
It is a blue hour, closing the bible.
Nothing is right in the world.
The only activity is the insects, startling with loudness,
making anguished illuminated half-light.
They inquire if I have suffered enough.
All I want is to be is forgiven.
There is nowhere in this world where I belong.

The Sculptor's Party
Jeremy Worman

In front of street lights London Plane trees shook in the wind. Through the studio's translucent blind patterns of stripped branches swerved over the floor. Laura stood in front of the Victorian cheval mirror as draughts ran up her thin legs.

'Getting on?' the sculptor called from upstairs.

'Almost done,' she shouted above the sound of Pink Floyd's new double album, *Another Brick in the Wall,* released last week.

He stood at the door, 'Thought you would have finished.'

'Getting ready.' She pulled down on her short black velvet dress. At the back of the studio her paintings stood like dominoes against the wall. She felt the shadow of her mother laughing at them.

'I'll hold the stepladders.'

'Bet you will. No fanks.'

They looked at each other.

Her teeth chattered, she put on the Fair Isle jumper, a Christmas present from her social worker. *Least she's not coming tonight, the way she looks at Nick, not letting him know straight, swishing her ass, flicking her hair. She ain't his type anyway.* Nick walked out. He spoke in her head—*Come on Laura, this is for you, get cracking*—better than some of the other voices. Just because he was an artist she didn't see why he liked paint all over his teeshirts. He looked nice in a proper shirt. She carried painting 'No 6' and hung it on the nail marked '6'. Half an hour later most were in place.

In the basement kitchen she made a strong mug of tea, stirred in two spoonfuls of sugar, and went to the junk room where she listened in the dark.

The fire hissed. She stacked on more wood then rolled up her sleeve: 'One, two, three—like sergeant's stripes.' The last cut was raised and purple. Her soldier ex-boyfriend had explained Army ranks by drawing them on her belly with a felt pen. He joined the Parachute Regiment and she never saw him after that.

The music stopped. Another voice, 'What an evening, it'll be fine / Life is lovely, life is mine, / Life is full of bubbly wine / This is 1979.' She laughed. Nick sang nonsense songs when he was happy. His soothing voice made her fingers dance. They touched her slashes. She closed her eyes and jerked her arm away. The hot mug warmed her hands. Nick was nice looking but too cocky, she wasn't going to just because he'd split with his girlfriend.

The flames shaped scenes from life in the Bermondsey flat: mother, brother, half brother, 'uncles'. They collected in the fireplace and their faces blocked the chimney. Nick rented rooms in his studio house. The couple on the third floor knew Laura's social worker. They had found her this place six months ago.

Tobacco and cigarette paper crumbled as she squeezed too tight, and she let it fall. *Snotty bitch from Social Services kept sending people to see we wasn't screwing.* 'Ha naw braun coww.' She watched her lips in the cracked wall mirror. She wanted to speak like Nick.

Tables and chairs scraped on the floor above as Nick arranged the studio. He had done the maquettes for Pink Floyd's Brick in the Wall Tour and one of the band was coming tonight. The mirror made faces as she put on mascara. And there was Nick, telling her to hurry up, as if they were going on a date. She made a cross in the patina of dust on a broken-legged mahogany table.

Banging made the basement shake. 'Fuckin' 'ell is that the time?' Saws, hanging from the beams, vibrated. She took off the jumper and brushed her long brown wiry hair. She adjusted her low-cut dress and unbolted the door. Nick stood there in black jeans, white shirt, blue corduroy cap.

'You look great,' he said.

'Not bad yourself, pity 'bout the shoes.' She stared at his off-white Greenflash.

'Bourgeois.'

'Scruffy git. Don't yer know what an iron is?'

There were three knocks. They ran up. Laura stood at the back and Nick opened the door. Her paintings were all over the studio and made her blush.

'Thanks for inviting me,' the soft female voice said.

Fucking shit. Laura bit the back of her hand.

Suzie Dyson, Laura's social worker, kissed Nick on both cheeks, and walked over to her. 'It's great you've done all this,' she said. Her long radiant blond hair touched Laura's cheek.

'Fanks.' Laura coughed and looked out of the window. *She smells like a fuckin' flower shop.*

Then she watched as Nick led Suzie to one of Laura's drawings and they talked la-di-da, 'Notice the fine details in the pattern,'

Nick said and Suzie added, 'I like how the figures change colour in sequence.' *Bollocks.* Laura put two fingers in her mouth and mimicked retching. *Don't fink you're going to get him, tart.*

'You seem very interested in art,' Nick said to Suzie.

'My father is an architect; he taught me how to look at things.' *Yeah, like Nick's crotch.*

Guests arrived. Fizzy wine bottles popped. 'The Indian are bringing food later,' Nick said as he turned up Pink Floyd. Laura poured wine for Suzie and managed to spit in the glass.

Propped on the ledge, her legs buckled as a crowd of her family shouted in her head. Her eyes blinked and tried to chase them away. The scars on her arm throbbed. Within an hour most of the guests had arrived. Then the food came and over twenty people tucked in. Laura pretended to eat, but didn't because she knew Indians put cats in the curry.

'I like the one where the girls look like sexy Daleks,' said a tall dark man with a big smile and an ankh dangling on his chest beneath an open blue psychedelic shirt.

Laura jumped. 'Yours for thirty quid, mate.'

'You were miles away. I'm Paul, a roadie with the Floyd.' He held out his hand.

'Pleased to meet yer,' she said as her eyes took him in. She glanced at a glossy man in the other corner, who everyone wanted to talk to but pretended they didn't. 'Is that...'

'Yeah,' Paul yawned nonchalantly.

Nick told her she had already sold three paintings and topped up her glass.

'If this carries on I'll be buying the fuckin' studio off you. Cheers,' she giggled.

Suzie was being chatted up by someone in a suede jacket and cowboy boots. *Stick wiv im, love, just right for an old scrubber like you.*

In the kitchen she ran the cold tap and the vibrating sound in the aluminium sink took away the other noises in her head. She drank a glass of water and picked up her fizzy-wine glass. Counting the bubbles, 'fifty, one hundred, two hundred', as they rose made her laugh—specks of froth went on forever. The basement door thudded shut behind her. The top hinge juddered. In the darkness the fireplace sucked at her. Cold air made goose bumps on her flesh. She counted the good-dream bubbles.

Nick came in and nudged her shoulder.

98

She recoiled.

'You're shivering.' He put his black elephant-cord jacket round her, then collected a few prints. They returned to the kitchen.

'Cheers.' She sipped and gave him the glass. He took a mouthful.

'Thanks for everything,' she said and gripped his arm. 'What clubs do yer like, then?'

'Dingwalls is my favourite, we can go if you want.'

'Love it. I'll treat yer with my earnings.'

'You keep your money.'

He pecked her on the cheek and walked out with his prints. Her cheek tingled. Still so much to learn about art. There were footsteps on the stripped wooden stairs as guests went up to the next floor. *The soldiers are retreating and leaving me alone.* Must be showing them his designs for the Pink Floyd tour, she realised and started to follow.

The basement door shook. She banged it and three loose rusty screws of the hinge stuttered back and forth. She slipped in again to the dark room, bolted the door, poked the smouldering ashes of the fire. *They're all laughin' at yer, Laura, with your la-di-da ways. And you know what Nick wants.* 'Get lost!' Laura screamed at the voice of her mother.

Her fingers stretched for the lamp switch, she tripped over a canvas, her glass slipped as liquid spilt—whoomph. The light came on and exploded. Objects swayed. Glass splintered across the floor. The bubbles were dying.

Laughter from upstairs became raucous. *Bet they're like that all the time, party to party, never alone in a basement.* She reapplied her makeup.

She glanced upstairs. That world felt so far away now. She sighed and made herself rejoin the party. Suzie and Nick were joking and laughing together. As Suzie reached behind him for a drink her cheek brushed his face. *Slag.*

Nick put on disco music and Laura danced with Paul, who said he would take her to a gig next week and Laura said maybe and lots of people chatted with her and praised her until most of them had left the party.

She touched each of her paintings, but they didn't belong to her anymore. She went downstairs. The music had stopped. Nick and Suzie were together in the studio. Laura made a cup of tea and tiptoed to the foot of the stairs. Suzie said, 'I'm following an

99

R.D. Laing theme about the falseness of labels and schizophrenia, post-Laing you know, but he led the way.'

'I read *Knots*,' Nick said.

'You've helped Laura so much.' She looked at him seriously. 'Art therapy is so underrated, have you read John Henzell's recent article by any chance?'

'Laura is coming along well, just needs a boyfriend,' Nick said. 'I don't think you've seen all the show yet. My maquettes are on the top floor.'

'Yes please.'

The mug was gripped so tight that her palms went red. The white kitchen was a waiting room and soon the nurse would say *Come in and see the psychiatrist now, he'll give you more drugs to keep you tame.* She crept up to the studio and took *Another Brick in the Wall.* In the basement junk room she lit a candle, played the album on the old record player, threw wood on the fire and knelt down. Her mother's angry face crouched among the flames. The small compass of light stretched just beyond the fireplace. She cupped her cheeks and tears wet her fingers. She lay down on the hard floor and listened: a silence over the house locked her out.

Later, the front door opened. 'Thanks for a lovely evening,' Suzie said.

A pause, not a snog pause, a few pecks on the cheek?

'Bye,' Nick said, 'thanks for coming.'

He skipped down to the basement.

'You okay?' he asked.

'Better now.'

He gave her a tissue and sat in the broken armchair. 'Want to go to Dingwalls next week?'

'If yer wear proper shoes.'

'Bourgeois.'

'Scruffy git.'

David Keyworth

Shift

You were both too lost in the low lighting
and racing to end each other's lines
to bother thanking the foreign waitress
who squeezed the blue candle between you.
Blurring buses flew at the speed of light
next to taxis clocking up the same velocity.
You were decoding each other's eyes
and feeling fusion shift the earth.

Next week, same table, you're waiting alone.
The shift manager crushes the guttering candle.
A cleaner critiques an essay on Einstein.
Outside late taxis are stranded at red.
The Roma waitress is on the last bus to Wythenshawe,
stopping, starting, crying,
beneath clouds and long-gone stars. 101

She Walked Through the Wall One Evening

Next evening I think I see her
by the warehouse, in the torn-off poster that

trips me, or the wind-kissed girl
stepping over the gap

between platform and tram.
Or is that her in the black coat,

a silhouette back-lit by the perfume billboard?
Is that her in the phone booth?

I follow her outline. I turn into the intimacy
of a moonlit alleyway.

Talking with Samuel Pepys about the Fire

I warm one hand on Americano steam,
try to place your address
on *The Independent's* map of the bushfire's rampage
(Why have we never exchanged e-mails?).
I'm getting nowhere.
Which is when Pepys appears.
He stumbles into the seat opposite.
I get him a latte, tap water and sandwich.
He asks if the vexatious wrapping is to keep out the plague
and where the musicians are hiding
and if this is a secret society,
if the Great Fire were the talk of the coffee-house,
if anything would outlive the flames.

I assure him that what we value most will survive.
He stares at me as if I were a madman.
Then he stands up,
gives me advice on digging a pit
for my parmesan and wine.
He takes one last breath of smoke-free air.
Says he must return to gather up his goods,
beneath the burning sky
and the sight of London, so sad.

I seal up my letter, which might
not reach you in Victoria.
Outside a black cloud is trying to drift   ·
away from a halo of sun.
Rain falls on the crumbs on the outside tables,
and into empty coffee cups.
It makes ink run on the famous names,
the birthday wishes, in the *Evening Standard*.

Noel Williams

Kim Phuc: The Song of Yellow Skin

When you see the flame the bomb has already fallen.
Earth has shifted irrevocably. Every bright bird is
caught, singing the song of Yellow Skin.

Napalm eats history, hope, all that is gold and green,
snatches the sun down to melt in Kim's nerves.
Now she can translate the unspeakable

each creak of her healing skin whispers of ash,
her cousins' only eulogy.
Her home, now veined with weeds

traps a black bird in concrete
fluttering in its ruin. She is crying
with the door shut, ragging feathers on cement.

Seven summers

Sucking sweet green blades.
My towel damp under me.
The Secret Seven.

Jeans greased by the chain,
I balance her birthday horse
on the handlebars.

Dead Man's Pool. The pole
hooked in mermaid weeds. We drift.
Willow flecks her eyes.

I breathe concrete, fold
my eyes under the sun's weight.
Gold stone. Fat brick. Noon.

A cocked flowerpot.
Buddleia snoring with bees.
A melted cat yawns.

Umbrellas roof our
barbecue in a hailstorm.
Steaks cooked by lightning.

A blackbird, a breeze,
the sudden pulse of roses.
Song my pen forgets.

In the Vice Provost's Garden

I follow a single leaf falling
(over the wall the hiss of horse chestnut
disapproves the bare hands of the breeze)
turning, in lime green as a slice of light,
falling past white walls, making me think
actually of not much, because it's obvious,
this single leaf falling, flickering thin
and then fat with the gift and loss of the sun,
what it might mean, if it was haiku;
or if it knew of Italians, Scots and Chinese
bright in the garden with lenses of hope,
posing and clicking to stretch this wonder
in a net under their future; or knew them
squealing with the delight of not drowning,
punted under a hundred summer bridges;
or guessed they built dykes with grains from the walls and towers
and ground from the river walks
to hold back the slide.

Which it can't. It's a single leaf,
endlessly not reaching the earth.

Litany

after Billy Collins, after Jacques Crickillon

You are the coal tongs that drag
the burning page out in time.

You are the song on my shoulder.

You are the hand that thrust me onto
the stage I'm going through.

You are where I'd like to be.

You are the chestnut in the tree,
tight in its spiked carapace
and I'm wondering how soon will it fall and split?

You are the deaf woman's crystal,
sounded with a fingernail.
You are fingernails, too, each rainbowed with an icon
from a muddy field heavy with guitars.

You are,
at least you think you are,
cornflowers on the roof.

You'd probably like to be the bread and the knife,
the white apron in pine scented air,
the basket of plums.
But you're not. One day, perhaps, you will be
the apron, the bread, the knife.
But, for the moment,
be the dew on the moon,
the boat burning in the sun.

Out Early
Adam Bayfield

Perhaps I shouldn't have saved the kid's life.

I guess I didn't realise just how paranoid everybody is these days. I worry for my own kids too, of course, but I wasn't fully aware of how hysterical other parents have become. Now I understand. My broken nose provides fairly unambiguous proof.

It started as a good day, better than usual because I left work early. The morning had passed agonisingly slowly; I ran down the clock by making coffee every fifteen minutes, filling the kettle to the top with cold water to prolong the time it took to boil. Bad for the environment, good for my sanity—less time spent relentlessly crunching numbers on the computer.

I don't know why I became an accountant, because I loathe numbers. At school I gave up numbers as soon as possible, at sixteen. Now, as I enter the September of my life, they're all I deal with. Actually, I do know why I became an accountant—for the salary. There's one set of figures I can stomach.

Time dragged interminably after lunch, but eventually the clock chimed two. As I rose to my feet and swung my tattered suit jacket over my shoulders, I could feel the envious eyes of my colleagues upon me.

'Where're you going, Edwards?' asked Phil Robinson, my desk neighbour, in his Illinois brogue. 'You know it's not clocking off time for another three hours?'

'My God, I wondered why it wasn't dark outside!' I replied in tones of mock surprise.

Robinson laughed. Before moving to the States, my compatriots had repeatedly informed me that Americans, being clinically unable to grasp irony, would fail to understand the crux of my sense of humour, but the three years I had spent here had taught me that this somewhat supercilious British belief was definitely a myth.

'I've asked for the afternoon off,' I continued, unable to stop myself smiling. 'I've got to pick the kids up from school'.

'Why, where's Kathy?' enquired Robinson.

The mention of my ex-wife transformed my smile into a dark frown.

'She and Chevy Chase, or whatever his name is, are indulging in a little romantic getaway in Minneapolis.'

'Good luck to them!' Robinson laughed again.

'How do you mean?'

'"Romance" and "Minneapolis" just don't really go together, Alex. Same as you wouldn't go to the Grand Canyon on a business trip, or go to Los Angeles expecting to feel anything other than crushing despair. Some things are incompatible.'

My mood brightened a little.

'Well anyway, the airport there was snowed in this morning, so their flight's a little late. I've gotta go get Evan and Lucy. I've not been to their new school yet; it's up in the Gold Coast. I've cleared it with HR.'

'Tough break, man.'

Now it was my turn to laugh.

'I know, I'll miss the boss' presentation this afternoon! Devastating.'

Returning Robinson's rueful glance with a gloating look of my own, I crossed the floor, signed myself out, took the elevator down the fifty-eight storeys to the lobby, and stepped out into the Chicago afternoon.

Cold air filled my lungs, expunging the recycled atmosphere of the office in an instant. The wind was icy, blowing through the little hole in the knee of my suit trousers and biting the exposed flesh. However, today the wintry weather felt more invigorating than disheartening.

I crossed Ohio Road to the bridge opposite my office block, from which you can see much of the city. It looked odd in the daylight. All the long winter I arrived at work in the dark and left in the dark. I'd forgotten how beautiful it was in the afternoon.

The sun was shining unimpeded through the cloudless sky, bathing Lake Michigan in a warm light that accentuated its deep, unadulterated blueness. The multitude of boats on the lake glowed incandescently in the afternoon sunshine, while the towering skyscrapers lining the shore reclined idly in their architectural resplendence, their impassive exteriors concealing the hives of activity and drudgery within.

Chicago is a delight before five. This is how tourists must see the city. Even the subway is pleasant. I normally only ride it during rush hour, when it is loathsome—the unmistakable stench of sweat and monotony; the violent jolts of the train; the flicker of shameful excitement when one of those jolts throws you into intimate proximity of an attractive woman. Today it was almost enjoyable.

Locating the school on leafy Texas Avenue was not difficult. Only moments after I arrived the bell rang, and, with the sort of immediacy I had always imagined was only possible in Hollywood high-school movies, the doors clattered open and children began pouring out into the playground, their excitable voices breaking shrilly on the air. I spotted Lucy quickly amongst the throng; she ran towards me, long blonde hair cascading around her shoulders, book bag dangling languidly at her side.

'Daddy!' she called breathlessly as she approached. 'What are you doing here?'

By way of response, I took three strides forward and swung her up into my arms.

'Mummy got held up in Minneapolis, sweetheart,' I beamed, 'so she asked me to take you guys home. Did you have a good day?'

'Oh yeah, great!' she replied, her eyes lighting up. 'We cut open a frog in science. It was gross! Amanda nearly fainted.'

'Sounds wonderful,' I chuckled. I felt so carefree during these precious, increasingly rare moments with my daughter. 'Where's your brother?'

'Oh, he won't be out for another fifteen minutes,' she said breezily. 'I always come out earlier than him. Didn't you know that?'

'What shall we do until then?'

'Can we play hide-and-go-seek?'

I winced at the Americanism. Lucy was only four when we moved Stateside and it had not taken long for her accent and vocabulary to adapt to her new surroundings. Not that I really minded.

'That sounds great. Stay in the playground though. Shall I be on?'

'No, I'm on! One, two, three...'

Kids must think adults can find hiding places with astonishing speed, for they always seem to hurry through the counting process rather rapidly. Filled with the childlike panic of someone who is running out of time to conceal themselves, I hared across in the direction of the first potential hiding place that leapt out at me, an oak tree on the perimeter of the playground. Dashing behind it just in time, I looked back to see Lucy remove her hands from her eyes, shout the word 'ten!', and scamper off in the opposite direction.

Crouching down as low as possible, I peered between a gap in the branches. My eyes were firmly fixed on Lucy, but I was confident she would be unable to see me. This one game might even use up the whole quarter of an hour before Evan came out.

A minute later, while Lucy was busy examining a Wendy house on the other side of the playground, I was overcome by the uncomfortable sensation of being watched. In the middle of the playground, a tall, pale woman was gazing over towards the oak tree with a puzzled expression on her face. Moments later, this transformed into a look of horror. Wrapping her arms around the boy standing at her feet, she leaned over to a burly man beside her and pointed animatedly in my direction.

Why was she so upset? I could not see anything unusual around me. Had we been in the mountains, I might have supposed there was a bear or a cougar in the tree, but in Chicago in January the only scary wildlife were the Saturday shoppers.

Then, suddenly, it hit me. What must this look like? A grown man, who had never been seen at this school before, skulking behind a tree, peering at the kids as they played happily in the playground. It could not look good.

By the time I had stood up and stumbled out into the playground both the man and the woman had begun to move at a purposeful pace towards the school building.

'Found you Daddy! That wasn't a very good hiding place!'

I wheeled round to see Lucy bouncing up and down beside me, wearing a triumphant grin.

'Now it's my turn to hide!' she exclaimed.

'I think that's enough of that game, Lucy,' I remarked through gritted teeth. 'Oh good, here comes your brother.'

Evan was making his way across the playground, a baseball cap perched precariously on his tousled mop of flaxen hair, and his shoulders drooping in a prematurely teenage slouch.

'Hello son,' I said.

'Hey Dad,' he replied. 'Mum not back yet?'

Aged nine when we moved over, Evan had retained all but the most peripheral vestiges of his Home Counties accent.

'The airport was snowed in this morning,' I muttered, 'we really ought to be going now.'

Evan eyed me suspiciously.

'Why do you look so flustered, Dad?'

'I'm fine Evan, it's just time to go, that's all.'

As we headed through the gates and out into the quiet street, I cast the occasional furtive glance behind me, but there was no sign of anyone following us.

'Aren't we going back to yours, Dad?' asked Evan, as we alighted the subway at Colorado Boulevard.

'No, your mother's flight should have landed by now, so she asked me to take you back home and wait with you there.'

'Awesome!' said Lucy. 'I can show you the doll Charlton bought me!'

Evan flashed his sister a stern look, but she seemed oblivious.

'It's really great! You can change its diaper and everything. Charlton always buys me things.'

'Lucy,' Evan groaned, 'don't talk about Charlton like that in front of Dad!'

Lucy stared at her brother for a moment.

'Oh don't worry Daddy, Charlton hasn't replaced you!' she said airily. 'You can still buy me things. He's just really nice. Like a second Daddy'.

Evan opened his mouth to scold his sister again.

'It's alright Evan,' I said gently. 'I don't mind.' I'm sure he knew I was lying, but, wordlessly, we agreed to let the matter drop.

Grey clouds were massing in the sky by the time we reached the apartment building where I had once resided with my family. The lobby, the stairwell, the elevators: a year ago they had all been friendly and welcoming, but now they seemed cold and remote.

Trusted latchkey kid that he is, Evan opened the apartment door. A delectable aroma and the sound of giggling emanating from the kitchen indicated that it was not empty.

'Hi kids!' came the call as soon as the door had closed behind us.

A moment later, Kathy bounded into the living room, enfolding both of our children in tight embraces.

'Oh I missed you two so much!' she said warmly. 'We just got in. Go and say hello to Charlton, he's missed you.'

The kids scuttled across the living room into the kitchen. There followed an awkward pause, as Kathy turned towards me. Her face was beginning to look hard and stern, lines were appearing around her wary green eyes, and little flecks of grey were starting to contaminate her soft, blonde hair, but my pulse

112

still quickened when she looked at me—she remained as beautiful as ever.

'Hello Alex,' she said, in a now-familiar detached voice. 'Thank you for getting them; I don't know what we'd have done otherwise.'

'My pleasure.'

Another awkward pause. The kitchen reverberated to the sound of laughter, prompting spikes of jealousy to sear within me. Evidently Charlton was engaging in some activity that my children found greatly amusing.

'How was Minneapolis?' I ventured.

'Oh, you know, not too bad. The hotel was lovely. Shame about the delay, but never mind. We both had good books.'

Yet another awkward pause. The silence seemed to hang about the room, snaking across the carpet I had once helped choose and wrapping itself around the plush furniture.

'Something smells good,' I said, unable to bear the quietude.

'Charlton's cooking quesadillas. One of his vegetarian recipes.'

Kathy looked me up and down. Suddenly I felt very exposed in the same threadbare suit I had been wearing for fifteen years.

'How's work?' she asked.

We had originally all moved to Chicago because Kathy's office had relocated her; once here, I had just taken the first job I could find. Perhaps she was hoping I would now move back home.

'Still the same,' I said simply, 'boring but bearable.'

The kitchen door burst open, and my ex-wife's new lover strode into the room, a smiling Lucy clinging to his muscular frame, and Evan trotting along at his heels.

'Alex! I didn't realise you were still here!' Charlton boomed in his confident Brooklyn accent.

He flashed me a sickening smile, his perfect white teeth glinting in the room's soft light. He looked imposing, almost regal, standing in front of the living room window's 20th-storey views of the city. During the divorce proceedings, Kathy had maintained that there was nobody else in her love life, but since only a month had passed between me moving out and Charlton moving in, I had drawn my own conclusions.

'Gee, if I'd known you were sticking around, I'd have made an extra quesadilla,' he said. 'How about staying for dinner?'

As he spoke, my eyes were drawn inexorably around the room to the numerous framed photographs of Charlton: in his bodybuilding gear, at the beach in his bathing suit, hugging my ex-wife and children. He looked horrifyingly handsome in all of them, his bright blue eyes shining up out of the pictures and piercing me like daggers. Anger bubbled in my chest.

'No, I'd better be going,' I said coldly.

'You're going out too though, aren't you darling?' said Kathy, gazing lovingly at Charlton.

'It's unfair, ain't it Alex? I cook the dinner, but I got no time to eat it. I've gotta go take a bodybuilding class. Hey, the gym's only two blocks from your apartment—maybe we could head over there together?'

'I'm not going home now, I'm going somewhere else,' I lied.

Bestowing final embraces on Lucy and Evan, I left the apartment and emerged back on Colorado Boulevard. The weather had taken a dramatic turn for the worse. Black clouds hung overhead and drops of rain were beating down on the tarmac in an unfaltering rhythm, while in the distance, the wind was beginning to whip up white horses on Lake Michigan. It was not yet sunset, but under the oppressive skies it was already gloomily dark. The street was awash with water, narrow streams connecting the dirty, brown puddles in a complex waterway of grime.

Stuffing my hands into my pockets, I traipsed back to the subway. The pavements were more or less empty, as people huddled in doorways to shield themselves from the rain, but the roads were as busy as ever, the endless procession of cars and taxis stirring up the puddles and spraying filthy water in all directions, including mine.

The rain had abated slightly when I came out of the subway onto Delaware Alley, but I was already soaked. Bitter thoughts swirled through my head as I trudged towards my dilapidated apartment building.

The sound of running footsteps snapped me abruptly out of my own mind. A boy of seven or eight sprinted past; his baggy clothes sodden from the rain. He was heading straight for a crossing up ahead, and did not appear to be slowing down despite the pedestrian light flashing a stern 'Don't Walk'.

'Hey!' I called, suddenly alarmed. The crossing teemed with speeding vehicles. Where were his parents?

Instinctively, I broke into a run, determined to overhaul the youth before he got himself killed. He was not going to stop.

114

What was he thinking? I had to get to him.

Just in time, I grabbed him by the arm and yanked him away from the edge of the road. A split-second later, a bus ploughed past. He would have been run down unceremoniously, but he seemed in no hurry to thank me. Instead, he struggled fiercely in my grip.

'Hey, get off me mister!'

'What the hell are you playing at?' I demanded. 'Do you want to get yourself killed?'

'Shut up! Stop touching me!'

'Wait just a minute young man...'

I was interrupted by the sound of a shriek breaking upon the air.

'What are you doing to my son?'

A tall woman was running up the pavement towards me, her ghostly white face contorted in a dreadful mixture of fear and rage. For a moment, I could not work out why I recognised her, and then, in one heart-stopping instant, it hit me: she had been at the school today. A shadow of fear passed across my own face.

'Get the hell away from my son!' the woman screamed.

'Hold on...' I began, but it was becoming abundantly clear that she had no intention of giving me a chance to explain myself.

I relaxed my grip on the boy's arm, and he staggered over to his mother, who continued to advance menacingly.

'You don't understand!' I said hurriedly, 'your son was about to run out into the road, and...'

'I know you!' she yelled. 'You were lurking at the school this afternoon! I went to get help but you'd slunk away by the time we came out!'

Many other pedestrians had now stopped in their tracks and were gazing at the scene in mingled interest and horror.

'Hey lady, what's going on?' one of them called.

'He's a paedophile!' she screamed, hysterical now. 'Paedophile! He was trying to snatch my son!'

'No, no, you've got it all wrong!' I shouted, panic seizing my vocal chords and raising my voice an octave.

The accusation was greeted by murmurs from the assembling mob.

Suddenly, my shoulder was taken in a vice-like grip. I wheeled round to reveal the burly man that had also been at the school earlier, his weathered face snarling.

'Jackson!' screeched the woman, looking triumphantly round at the crowd. 'My husband will protect us!'

Before I could react, he had swung his fist. My nose broke instantly. Blood spurted down my front as I stumbled backwards and fell to the ground. Waves of nauseating pain washed over me, one after another.

The big man bent down, grabbed me by my blood-stained collar, and raised his huge fist again.

'Get him, Jackson!' I heard the woman shriek, though she seemed distant now.

I shut my eyes.

But no blow landed. He had not struck me again.

Blearily, I opened one eye. My assailant was on his feet, being held back against his will by an even bigger man, who had evidently intervened. It did not take me long to recognise this new arrival, either.

'Stand back everyone!' Charlton instructed loudly.

Pushing my attacker to one side, he moved over to me.

'You look a mess, Alex,' said Charlton. 'I don't know what you did, but we oughtta get out of here—these people seem pretty mad.'

Wrapping his brawny arms around me, he hauled me to my feet, and offered me support as I swayed unsteadily, the blood still streaming down my front.

Two men, including my assailant, started towards us.

'I wouldn't if I were you,' warned Charlton, and, intimidated, they backed off. 'Come on; let's get you to a hospital.'

'He's getting away, Jackson! We can't let him get away!' screamed the woman as Charlton more or less dragged me along the street, but nobody appeared to follow us.

'What the hell did you do to get them all riled up like that?' Charlton asked.

In the clipped sentences of one who has broken a tender part of their anatomy, I explained.

'So this nose is what I get for saving a kid's life,' I finished. Charlton chuckled.

'They definitely overreacted, although hiding like that was a dumb thing to do. Lucky for you I took this route to my class.'

Charlton hailed a taxicab, and we proceeded in silence to the hospital. He stayed with me while my nose was patched up.

'Well, I oughtta get going,' he remarked as we walked out the hospital doors into the Chicago night, 'Kathy will be wondering where I am.'

I looked away from him as he said this.

'I'll straighten things out with the school tomorrow,' he continued, 'explain who you are and what you were doing. It'll all be fine.'

There was a pointed pause.

'Look,' he said, 'I know how difficult it's been for you Alex, I do. But things could be easier, if only you allowed them to be.'

I tried to speak but the words stuck in my throat.

'It's time to move on buddy. Kathy doesn't love you anymore —and I don't think you love her either.'

I raised my eyes to meet his.

'You're a good dad, Alex. I really believe that. Kathy does too; hell, why do you think she asked you to look after the kids today? She trusts you. And Evan and Lucy love you like anything. They talk about you all the time. They're great kids.'

Raw emotion surged in my chest, and I felt suddenly tearful.

'They are, aren't they?' I said.

There followed a long pause. Charlton placed his hand on my shoulder.

'Take care of yourself, Alex.'

With that, he marched away up the street, his big stride enabling him to step effortlessly over the puddles on the sidewalk.

I watched him until he had disappeared around a corner, and then set off in the opposite direction. When I reached California Avenue, I stopped to look at the Chicago skyline. The rain had subsided, and the city sparkled with lights. The shore of Lake Michigan was illuminated, but the majority of its boundless, enveloping immensity was as black as the night sky above it.

My heart soared with love for this city. Boring job, broken nose. Never mind. I thought of Evan and Lucy. Chicago is their home. And it's mine now too.

Sharon Black

Firmament

I Cosmonaut

You wear the moon like a glove
that has been draped over the back
of my mind all day. You wear it
so well, I don't even feel your hand
sliding over, into, through me —
as if I were the ghost of your beloved
grandmother, your hell-bent cousin
with the beautiful singing voice,
your mute maiden aunt who died
wearing only *mousquetaires*
after slipping from her sill
one bright, sloping night.

II Supernova

and when you slant across my belly
and a sister-pulse flutters
deep in my groin,
I breathe in the stars, loosen
their constellations in my mouth
and balance their orbits
on the tip of my tongue,
to stop myself

III Nebula

The hours steal away, some
unlatching the window, spreading
their wings in the cool air;
some through cracks in lath and plaster;
some riding out on white horses—
bold as the moon, and shining.

IV Eclipse

and later, when you lift
your body from mine
and drift into the night,
I wrap myself in your shadow,
layering it round me
tighter and tighter
until I all but disappear

Breakwater

In the middle of a gallery
I've wandered into to avoid the rain
in a smart Parisian *quartier,*
I find you wanton and dreaming,

reclining in the Firth of Clyde—
naked but for the isle of Arran
knuckled across your right breast; the dark mole
of Ailsa Craig midway down your *linea alba;*

a faint track of scars marking
underwater contours;
a single score of latitude. Your belly
skims the Ayrshire coastline,

its stretch marks catching in the sun
like silvery eels;
your pubic thatch is a shoal of fish
tugging on the current.

Both nipples are adrift—one nudging
the gentile seaside town of Troon,
the other its own unmapped island
cocked towards Kintyre.

Elbow thrown back
above your tipped-back head, fist
plunging the depths of Loch Fyne,
the Sound of Jura in your ears,

you hold back tides and wait,
warm as stone,
for rusting herring trawlers and the lonely nets
of wind-beaten fishermen.

Sepia

Hard to tell where body ends and land begins:
this coastline mapped in tendons and arteries,
in erogenous zones and stretch-marks,
your moon-curves pushing back landslide, bays and cliffs,
these wrinkled, flaking edges
that could crumble
like parchment under my hands.

Strand

You wear your body like a scroll—
your past laid out in nautical miles,
your present etched
with grid coordinates, latitude, place
names I've never heard of,
each muscle tensed, each sinew pushed
proud of Earth's crust, pectorals pulled
tight as a footbridge
I've been waiting on the other side of for years.

Garden of Antipathy
Lindsay Stanberry-Flynn

'I think we should meet.' Rose's voice came down the receiver, aggressive, demanding, as if she, not Marnie, had scores to settle.

Marnie hooked the phone under her chin, while she drew the cake from the oven. The buzz of the timer had coincided precisely with the ringing of the phone. 'Do you? Why?' She pressed her finger against the top of the sponge. Watched the small hollow, waiting for it to spring back. The indentation remained.

'We need to clear the air. Get our friendship back on track.'

Marnie didn't answer. She opened the oven again and shoved the cake back in. She slammed the door shut.

'What's that noise? Are you listening to me?' Rose's questions scratched at Marnie's ear.

'Sort of. My cake's getting spoilt.'

'For heaven's sake, Marnie! You can buy a cake from Waitrose. This is important.'

'I'm baking a cake for Jamie's birthday. *That's* important.'

Rose sighed a determined sigh. 'But Jamie's coming to us for his birthday. You agreed it last week.'

'I've changed my mind.'

'His father will be devastated.' Rose's voice rose to a screech.

Marnie remembered Jamie's father's devastation when their second baby—a daughter with a shock of black fluffy hair—died before they could name her. How much devastation could one man take? She reset the timer.

'This isn't getting us anywhere,' Rose said. 'We've got to meet.'

'Right.' Marnie felt the cry of battle whoop in her chest, like a child stashing his pirate's cutlass under the pillow, to slay the dragon who taunted his nights. 'When?'

'Oh—you mean you'll come?'

Marnie stared at the numbers ticking down on the timer. 'I thought that was what you wanted.'

'Well—it is—but I didn't think you'd say yes today.'

'I'll tell you what...' Through the glass of the oven door, Marnie saw the surface of her cake was plump and golden. 'Phone again tomorrow and I'll agree then.'

'Don't be like that, Marnie. This isn't easy for either of us.'

Easy? Fuck easy! Easy! Fuck you, Rose! Marnie never swore, but the bite of the 'f' on her lower lip, the firecracker 'k' reverberating round her mouth, down into her throat, through her chest and into her belly made her want to shout the word down the phone line, shout it, scream it, like a demented fishwife.

'Are you still there, Marnie?'

It didn't seem fair—who first gave fishwives their shrewish reputation? Was there once a wife who waited and waited for her husband to arrive home from weeks at sea, who waited for the riches of the catch to put food on the table, who waited for her fisherman to return to her bed, who waited for his strong body to wrap itself round hers, for his voice, cracked by harsh winds, to whisper into her ear... only for the words 'I love another' to worm themselves into her brain?

Did that fisherwoman scream, as the fisherman removed his arms from round her, withdrew his voice from her ear, unpicked his heart from hers?

'Marnie, don't go all silent. Say something.'

Marnie squeezed the receiver, as if she could cut off its breath. 'The buzzer's going. Just tell me when you want to meet.'

'You'll definitely come?'

Marnie eased the cake tin from the oven. 'Yes.'

'Tomorrow. Eleven o'clock.'

'Where?'

'Elsa's,' Rose said.

'The teashop?'

'Well, of course the teashop!'

Marnie glanced out of the window at the rain slicing diagonally across the patio, at Jamie's empty swing bouncing and cavorting in the restless wind. Elsa's? Where they'd ordered tea and pastries on Mondays after Spanish; soup and a roll on Wednesdays after keep fit; where Rose murmured the word 'infertile'; where Marnie said 'I drink'; where Rose confessed she didn't love her husband any more; where Marnie wondered if Jamie's father was having an affair.

'No,' she said. 'Not Elsa's.'

The telephone wires drooped with the weight of Rose's impatience. Marnie could imagine her complaining to Jamie's father over dinner, 'I don't know how you put up with her for so long. You're a saint.'

124

'Where then?' Rose snapped.

Marnie pictured a wasteland of ice: where the wind would bite into Rose's cheeks and redden them, the frost would eat into her fingers and burn them, the cold would seep into her soul and damn her. 'Somewhere outside,' she said.

'Oh, I see.' Rose's tone had brightened—at last they were making progress. 'Neutral territory. Good idea.'

She paused and Marnie could almost see her checking her list of 'possible places of neutral territory'.

'I don't know why I didn't think of it before,' she announced, with all the delight of Archimedes. 'The Garden of Remembrance.'

'Remembrance?' The cake nearly slipped from Marnie's grasp.

'You know, in the High Street. They've replanted it with all white flowers. We took Jamie there last Sunday. It's perfect.'

Marnie recalled Sunday's exhausted hours, while Jamie was with his father and Rose. 'Yes,' she said. 'I can see. Perfect.'

Come and share the joy of our refurbished Garden of Remembrance

A place to think of friend and foe

A place our dreams to tend and sow

A place to meet for you and me

A place to find tranquility

Marnie stopped at the entrance to the garden and her eyes flitted over the rhyme on the board inside the gate. The new black paint shone glossily on its white background: you, me, friend, foe —it was as if Rose had been here in the dead of night, paintbrush in hand, appropriating the board's message for today's meeting. On second thoughts, she wouldn't have left Jamie's father in bed on his own—he might have got cold, poor thing, or lonely, or worse, he might have escaped while her back was turned.

'Lovely, aren't they?' The voice came from somewhere near Marnie's left shoulder. 'I read them words every day.'

Marnie looked round. The woman wore a brown coat and a black beret pulled down over tightly-permed hair. 'It's ten years since my Bill went.' She dabbed at her eyes with a white handkerchief. 'But you don't get used to it.'

'I suppose not,' Marnie said.

'You on your own?' The woman's mouth was a gash of the

pearly pink she must have been wearing since she was a teenager.

On your own. Alone. Isolated. Insular. Secluded. Abandoned. Marnie had spent one sleepless night counting how many words she knew for alone. Next morning she thought of solitary. 'Number one is a solitary number,' her maths teacher used to say. 'You can have fun with other numbers—add them, divide them, make patterns. But number one is—'

'What about halves and quarters, Miss?'

'They're fractions, aren't they, Marnie?' Miss's voice held that last-thing-on-Friday-afternoon note. 'They're not whole.'

'Yes,' Marnie said now, remembering that she wasn't whole any more. 'I'm on my own.'

'I've got Molly, of course,' the woman said. 'Lovely little tabby, she is. Sleeps on my bed, but it's not the same, is it?'

Marnie thought of the nights when Jamie woke, when a nightmare made him tremble, when he'd climb into her bed and she'd cuddle his bony frame. He'd cling to her neck and his hot breath would blow in her face. 'I want Daddy,' he'd cry. 'When's Daddy coming home?'

'No, it's not the same,' she agreed.

Despite the hankie, the woman's eyes watered the powder on her cheeks.

'Trust you to be early!' A second voice addressed itself to Marnie—this time not the soft, pliable quality of the woman in the black beret, but Rose's more querulous tone. Marnie pushed her hands into her jacket pockets and turned round.

'You know you're never early, Marnie.' Rose's cheeks were flushed, and there was a pimple on her chin. 'Why do you have to be early today?'

Marnie bunched her fingers into fists. 'Perhaps I should ask why you're late.'

Rose's pimple seemed to grow redder and angrier as Marnie stared at it.

'I'm not,' she insisted. 'The clock was striking eleven as I came along the road.'

Marnie glanced towards the woman in the beret. 'I didn't hear the clock, did you?'

'No dear, but then my hearing's not very good. My Bill always said—'

'For heaven's sake, Marnie!' Rose stalked towards the gate of the garden. 'Let's get on with it. I've got to be at the hairdresser's at midday.'

Marnie touched the woman's arm. 'It was nice to meet you. I'd better go.'

'That's all right, dear. You don't want to keep your friend waiting.'

'Oh, she's not my friend.'

Marnie followed Rose along one of the paths to a bench at the far end of the garden. She would have liked to look at the flowers. She and Jamie's father had made a garden together once, poring over books, plotting out the beds, grieving for plants that died, celebrating ones that blossomed. But that was a long time ago. She glanced around her: white clematis was growing through the arms of a tree, a dicentra's bell-shaped flowers arched on their stems, delicate white cyclamen crouched on the earth, bridal wreath... oh no... bridal wreath spirea, the fountain of white flowers like a mound of snow. It was one of the first plants they'd bought: 'to remind us of the best day of our lives,' Jamie's father had said. 'A tough plant—will tolerate cold exposed locations,' the label read.

'Come on, Marnie.' Rose beckoned from the bench. 'There's a lot to talk about.'

Marnie sat down and waited. She stared straight ahead at a patch of daffodils, left over from earlier in the spring, their once-jaunty blooms shrivelled. The scent of Rose's perfume held her rigid. Love in the Mist—it was the one she'd worn since Marnie had bought it for her birthday. Marnie breathed in its peachy fragrance. She closed her eyes. How could Rose still smell the same? The same as when they'd sat next to each other at the cinema? The same as when they'd stood together in the choir? The same as when she'd lain beside Marnie in the park in summer sunshine?

'Say something.' Rose's voice stabbed her reverie.

Marnie opened her eyes and forced herself to look at Rose. Rose was smiling. Her front tooth had been fixed. The one that had had a chip ever since she'd fallen in the school playground was now smooth, complete, its wondrousness outshining all the other teeth.

'You've had your tooth done,' Marnie said.

Rose batted her hand at the air, as if she might flick away Marnie's comment.

127

'I suppose Jamie's father suggested it,' Marnie said. 'He never could cope with imperfection.'

It was Rose's turn to look away. Marnie followed her gaze—it wasn't on the withered daffodils but turned upwards to the branches of the lime tree arcing overhead, slivers of steely sky edging between them. Perhaps that was the problem: Marnie's gaze forever down and in; Rose's up and out. Perhaps that was what Jamie's father had chosen.

'I thought we were going to try and put things right,' Rose said.

'Did you? And how do you propose doing that?'

Rose's fingers tightened over the clasp of her red handbag. 'We'll pick up the pieces, mend them... there must be some way.' Rose glanced about her, as if the clematis, the paving stones, even the fountain trickling its thin stream of water might provide the inspiration for this tricky mending problem

Marnie pictured the blackbird that had flown into the kitchen window last week. It had lain on the patio, its terrified heart pulsating under its puffed-up chest. Its eyes had stared unblinkingly at her as she bent down to examine its mangled wing. It had happened once before, when Jamie's father still lived there. He had picked the dying bird up on his spade and carried it to the bottom of the garden. Marnie had heard the thwack of the spade against the ground. 'What was I supposed to do?' he'd protested later when she cried. 'You've got to put the thing out of its misery.' Marnie had refilled her glass of wine.

'It's not like a broken vase, Rose,' she said now. 'You can't glue the bits together and turn the joins to the back of the shelf.'

'You don't even want to try to put things right, do you?' Rose sniffed loudly, something she'd always done when she thought she'd had the last word.

'What would you do?' Marnie asked. 'If you were me?' It was a game they'd always played. Failed exams, being dumped by boyfriends, rows with parents—all made less painful by 'What would you do?' Sharing possibilities—custard pie in Mr Smith's face? Itching powder in the ugly fart's jeans? A note saying you'd run away to sea?—and they'd clutch each other, rocking with laughter. Did Rose remember those times? Was that why she blinked when Marnie asked, 'What would you do?'

'I'd let Jamie come to us for his birthday, for a start.'

'And you'd sit at home on your own on your son's sixth birthday?'

'If it meant Jamie was happy.'

'And coming to you would make Jamie happy?'

Rose's eyes glinted. She must have been sensing success. 'Of course. Jamie adores his father. All little boys do.'

Marnie stood up. 'He's not coming to you for his birthday, Rose. If Jamie's father wants to be with him, tell him he can come for tea.'

'At your house?' Rose's voice reached up into her scalp.

'Yes.'

'But he can't come to you! What about me?'

'What about you, Rose?'

On the way home, Marnie bought candles and balloons and a shiny silver banner with 'Have a great day' printed across it in letters of glittering green. She bought chocolate biscuits and jelly and ice cream and party poppers and a box of indoor fireworks. At home, she iced the cake and wrote, 'Happy Birthday Jamie 6 today' in blue icing. She wrapped up his presents, a remote-controlled racing car and a superman outfit. When it was almost time for Jamie to come home from school, she hid everything until the next day.

She went into her bedroom, the one she'd shared with Jamie's father, and pulled down the case from the top of the wardrobe. She folded in shirts and jumpers, jangling hangers left empty; she pulled the pyjamas from under his pillow, pyjamas she'd cuddled to herself when she couldn't sleep, and threw them into the case. She put in their wedding photo that had stood on the chest of drawers on Jamie's father's side of the bed; and she added the bottle of his aftershave that she'd allowed herself to smell on bad days.

Jamie was at the table eating fish fingers and baked beans, when the phone rang.

Marnie's eyes went to the clock: six. 'That'll be Daddy, Jamie. Take it in the lounge.'

'Daaaaaaaddy!' Jamie's cry bounced off the walls in the hall.

Marnie stood at the kitchen window and stared out into the evening gloom. Jamie's bike was lying on its side in the middle of the lawn. Washing, wet from the afternoon's downpour, moped on the line. Marnie hummed to herself, but still snatches of Jamie's chatter got through: tomorrow... presents... Daddy... tea.

129

It had gone quiet. Jamie was tapping her on the arm. 'Daddy says can he come to tea tomorrow.' His eyes, dark and serious, just like his father's, stared up at her.

She ran her hand over his hair, combing it back from his eyes with her fingers. 'For your birthday?'

'He can, can't he, Mummy? Please say he can.'

'Of course he can. Tell him to come about half past five.'

Jamie's forehead creased. 'When the little hand's on five and the big hand's on six?'

'That's right. Well done.'

'And also Mummy…'

'Yes?'

'Daddy said—can he stay the night.'

A fist closed round Marnie's heart. For a moment she thought she'd stopped breathing and she forced her lungs to work—in, out, in, out.

'Please say yes, Mummy.'

Marnie looked away from his brooding stare. 'No, I'm sorry, Jamie. He can't.'

Jamie pulled on her sleeve. 'Please.'

She crouched down until her face was level with his. She caught hold of his hands and gripped them between her own. 'He can come for tea. But not to stay.'

Jamie stuck out his bottom lip. 'Next week then. Can he come next week?'

Marnie thought of the packed suitcase sitting in the bedroom —the last of Jamie's father's belongings. 'For tea, but not to stay.' Never again to stay.

'It's not fair!'

'No, it's not fair,' Marnie said. *Nothing is fair.* 'But you can go and see Daddy sometimes.'

Jamie screwed up his nose. 'I don't want to go there any more. I hate Auntie Rose.'

Hate. Such a small word. Other four-letter words were forbidden. But they rose like bile into Marnie's throat. 'Okay,' she said. 'Then maybe you and Daddy could go out somewhere together?'

'Just me and him?'

'Why don't you ask? Go on—he's still on the end of the phone, isn't he?'

Jamie whirled out of her arms so fast, a draught passed over her face. She heard him shouting and whooping along the hall.

She stood up and stared out into the garden again. The next-door neighbour's security light had come on, sending a shaft of luminous silver across the darkness. There was movement out there. She could just make out the branches of the buddleia half way along the garden swaying. The shapes on the line flapped and flew. A wind had got up. The washing might be dry in the morning.

Contributors

Adam Bayfield

Annie Bien is delighted her poems are included in this anthology. Her poetry and fiction have appeared in magazines and online publications. Her first writing commission was from the Soho Theatre Company, London, England. She is an editor for the American Institute of Buddhist Studies at Columbia University, New York.

Sharon Black is originally from Glasgow but now lives in the remote Cévennes Mountains of southern France. In her former life she was a journalist. In her current one she organises holiday courses that include creative writing (www.gardoussel.com). In 2009 she won the *Envoi* poetry prize and *The New Writer* prize for Best Single Poem, also taking 2nd prize in the latter's Poetry Collection category. She has been published in various magazines and anthologies including *Mslexia, Envoi* and *Aesthetica* and has been shortlisted four times for the Cinnamon Press Poetry Collection Award.

Jacci Bulman is studying for an M.A. in Poetry at Manchester University. She has had work published in South Bank magazine and was short-listed for the 2010 Bridport Prize. Her greatest inspirations have been a group of children she met in Vietnam, healing, and the poetry of Raymond Carver. She lives in an old chapel in the Eden Valley.

Lezanne Clannachan is thirty-seven years old, was born in Denmark and has lived in Brazil, Poland and Singapore. She is currently in West Sussex with her husband and three young children where she runs a local writing group. She is completing her first novel *The Cuckoo-Clock Bride*.

Barbara Cumbers lives and works in London. Her poems have appeared in a number of magazines and anthologies. She is currently working on a first collection.

Natalie Donbavand

Claire Dyer writes women's fiction and works part-time for a London-based HR research forum as well as writing poetry. She was commended in the 2010 Ware Open Poetry Competition and won the 2010 WomenWords poetry competition. She has had poems published by *Orbis, Ragged Raven Press, Envoi* and Leaf Books.

David Gill was born and raised in Cumbria. He studied Philosophy and Literature at Warwick University, and then taught English before becoming the head-teacher of a comprehensive school. He is currently an education adviser. David lives in the East Midlands with his wife and sons.

Ayesha Hebl

Will Kemp studied at Cambridge and UEA, then travelled throughout Asia and South America before working as an environmental consultant in Holland, Canada and New Zealand. Since becoming runner-up in the Keats-Shelley Prize 2006, he has had over fifty poems published and shortlisted in various national journals and competitions.

David Keyworth was born in West Bromwich in 1971, but grew up mainly in North Lincolnshire. He lived in Worcester for ten years. His job is based around Manchester and he is a Chair of the POETICA group. He has been published in *Smiths Knoll, Orbis, Rain Dog, Obsessed with Pipework* and elsewhere.

Kaye Lee is an Australia, living in North London. Since retiring from nursing Lee has been able to concentrate on writing and has had some poems published in small press magazines and anthologies. Lee has been a prize-winner or shortlisted in several competitions.

Patrick Lodge worked as a lecturer and manager in English higher education, He has always written for personal pleasure, but early retirement gave him the space and time to focus on writing. He spends as much time travelling as possible and many of his poems derive from a particular observed scene and tthemes of memory and change. He holds dual Irish and British citizenship and the tensions and possibilities of this inform his work. He lives in Yorkshire.

John Mackay was born in South Yorkshire, and has worked as a journalist and teacher. He is currently studying for a PhD in contemporary American elegy at Birkbeck College, London. He has had work published in magazines, anthologies, and books about personal writing,

Phil Madden lives in Abergavenny, but travels extensively across Europe as a consultant supporting people with disabilities. His Poster Poems were recently exhibited at a gallery in Brussels. He is working on a book of poems and wood engravings about birds with the award winning engraver, Paul Kershaw.

Rosemary Mairs has been awarded numerous prizes in short story competitions, and she won the prestigious Society of Authors' Tom Gallon Award in 2009. She has also previously been published in the 2008 Cinnamon Press Short Story Award anthology. She lives in County Antrim, and is currently working on a novel.

Isabella Mead works as a methodology trainer for teachers in Rwanda. She has been published in many magazines, including *Poetry News* and *Envoi*, and has been shortlisted for awards including Eric Gregory Award 2009, Bridport Prize 2008 and Templar Pamphlets 2010.

Julie Mellor is a graduate of Sheffield Hallam's MA Writing. She has had work published in *Brittle Star, The Nerve* (Virago), *London Magazine* and *Mslexia*. She currently teaches English at a secondary school in Barnsley.

Sue Moules has appeared in three previous Cinnamon anthologies—*The Ground Beneath Her Feet, The Visitors* and *Glimmer*. Her poems have appeared in *Poetry Wales, New Welsh Review, Planet, Roundyhouse and The Interpreter's house*. Her most recent collection is *The Earth Singing* (Lapwing) 2010.

Marcus Smith is Cinnamon Press finalist. His work has appeared in *Ambit, Acumen, PN Review, Prairie Schooner, Salzburg Poetry Review* and *The South Carolina Review*.

Lindsay Stanberry-Flynn taught English in further and higher education before giving up to concentrate on writing. She has an MA in creative writing from Bath Spa University. Her first novel, *Unravelling*, was published in June 2010, and she is currently revising a second, *The Piano Player's Son*. Her short stories have been successful in competitions such as The Fish International Short Story Prize and the Asham Award for Women Writers. In 2009 'The Magic of Stories' appeared in the anthology *Storm at Galesburg* published by Cinnamon Press. Lindsay lives in Worcestershire where she teaches creative writing.

Aisling Tempany is a young Cardiff-based poet currently working on a part-time English masters at Swansea University. This will be her fourth appearance in Cinnamon's anthologies, after *Storm at Galesburg*, *The Visitors* and *Glimmer*. She has recently appeared in *Orbis* (153)

Nicola Warwick lives in Suffolk and works in local government. She has had poems in several magazines, including *The Rialto, Smith's Knoll* and *Equinox*, as well as prizes and commendations in various competitions.

Noel Williams is widely published in anthologies and magazines including *The North, Orbis, Envoi* and *Iota*. As Resident Poet at Bank Street Arts Centre in Sheffield his exhibition Exploding Poetry filled five gallery spaces, attracting 400 visitors. He's won many commendations and prizes, including the Wasafiri Prize, the Yorkshire Prize, finalist in Aesthetica Creative Works and runner up in the Troubadour. See: http://noelwilliams.wordpress.com/

Martin Willitts Jr poems appear in *Storm at Galesburg and other stories* (international anthology). His tenth chapbook is *The Garden of French Horns* (Pudding House Publications, 2008) and his second full length book of poetry is *The Hummingbird* (March Street Press, 2009. He is co-editor of www.hotmetalpress.nert

Jeremy Worman has reviewed for *The Observer*, *The Sunday Telegraph*, *The Spectator*, the *New Statesman*, the *TLS* and many other publications. His short stories and poems have been published widely. *Fragmented*, an autobiographical collection of stories about London, is forthcoming with Cinnamon Press. He is editorial advisor for *The London Magazine* and teaches English Literature to American students at Birkbeck College, London University. Jeremy is represented by literary agent: Christopher Sinclair-Stevenson. www.jeremyworman.com